Haynes

Build your own Electric Guitar

Haynes Publishing

'Making the simple complicated is commonplace; making the complicated simple, awesomely simple, that's creativity.'
Charlie Mingus

First published in January 2013

A catalogue record for this book is available from the British Library

ISBN 978 0 85733 258 5

Library of Congress catalog card no. 2012944796

Published by Haynes Publishing,
Sparkford, Yeovil, Somerset BA22 7JJ, UK

Tel: 01963 442030 Fax: 01963 440001
Int. tel: +44 1963 442030 Int. fax: +44 1963 440001
E-mail: sales@haynes.co.uk
Website: www.haynes.co.uk

Haynes North America, Inc.,
861 Lawrence Drive, Newbury Park,
California 91320, USA

Printed in the USA by Odcombe Press LP,
1299 Bridgestone Parkway, La Vergne, TN 37086

Build your own
Electric
Guitar

Paul Balmer

Foreword by **Brian May**

Contents

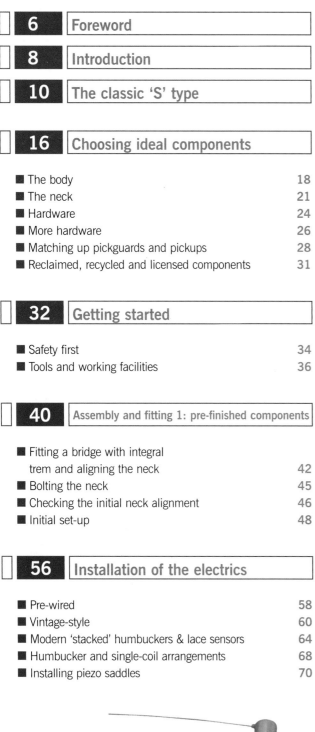

Foreword

The 'Red Special' I play was an experiment really. My Dad was a quite brilliant man, he could turn his hand to anything; electronics, metalwork, woodwork – he had an amazing instinct for things and he taught me some of that. We built it because we couldn't afford 'a real one' and also it could be something no-one else had.

I'd played around with my friend's guitars; Hofners' and imitation Stratocasters, Watkins Rapiers, and so I knew their faults and thought 'I can make something better than that!'

It became a very personal instrument; the buttons used for position markers and the knitting needle tip came from my Mum, the saddle bag arm is off my bike. The body is partly hollow and it's the first guitar I'm aware of built with feedback as a goal rather than a nuisance.

We had lots of hand tools – planes, chisels and sandpaper, though we didn't have any power tools. I think a penknife was used near the nut, and the neck was certainly a piece of a fireplace.

When the guitar was assembled, I hooked it up to my Dad's radio, and I had all the wires hanging out, and I thought, 'well what do I do?' So I came up with an 'on' and 'off' for each pickup and a phase reversal for each pickup, and then I could get a lot of different sounds. They are all wired in series, not in parallel, because it was a bit warmer sounding that way.

It's much easier now to obtain guitar parts and so maybe I would do things differently, but the 'Red Special' is still my first-choice guitar. Good luck with making your own guitar!

Dr. Brian May CBE
June 2012

Introduction

This book is aimed at first-time guitar builders. Though I've maintained and repaired many guitars I've never before built one before – so we're in this together! Fortunately we're being guided and corrected by master luthiers John Diggins and son Andy, who've been building guitars for Tony Iommi, AC/DC and Mark King for half a century, so we're in good hands.

Together we agreed that the easiest way into the world of electric-guitar making is to assemble and 'fit' an 'S' type. As few of us have access to the complex routers and jigs required for wood shaping I'm assuming the body and neck are obtained pre-cut, and we'll focus our energies on the important and fascinating issues of accurate assembly, finish, pickup choices and set-up. This will engage us with all the primary factors contributing to good guitar making, and should give us a good working guitar first time!

We follow here in the well-trodden footsteps of Eric Clapton, whose 'bitsa' Blackie is one of the world's most famous guitars.

I hope some of you will be inspired by these projects to go the extra mile and start another instrument from raw uncut wood, with the investment in tools and workspace which that involves. I hope most of us will learn enough to better understand our guitars and consequently get more from them.

The 'S' type is a classic, played since 1954 by everybody from Buddy Holly to Jimi Hendrix to the Red Hot Chilli Peppers. In looks it's the Ferrari Testarossa, and for sound it offers everything from clean elegance to screaming passion.

John and Andy Diggins – luthiers.

Though the 'S' type emerged from the mass-production processes of the 1950s and lends itself to a DIY approach, this isn't about making a cheap guitar or undercutting existing suppliers; my instinct is that if you're going to build your own 'S' type you should build a good one – as did Eric. It will involve buying quality, not cheap, parts and investing many constructive and pleasurable hours learning new skills.

You may already own a Far Eastern copy 'S' type, and they're great value. The current stock American guitar is also excellent, and a worthy tribute to its genius development team. It's interesting how many guitarists with potentially unlimited budgets still return to this simple classic guitar when all else has been explored.

What this book does offer is something slightly more – the chance to custom-build your own, individual classic with all the right ingredients for you, from prime tone woods to your chosen pickups, from 'vintage' spec to 'Texas Specials'.

The original brilliant design concept makes the 'S' type easy to assemble and very player-friendly, but the professional 'fitting' – how you put the components together – is critical to success. A poorly assembled guitar is a useless piece of junk, whilst a well set-up one opens the door to endless musical possibilities. I'll guide you through the essential steps that will make your guitar a 'goer', from choosing appropriate timber to making choices about the sound you want from your very individual instrument.

Start with some knotty ash.

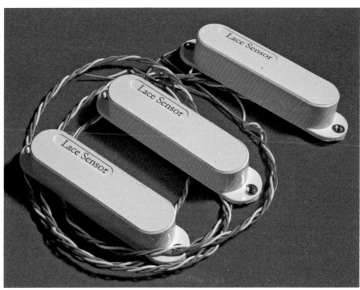

The basic design of the 'S' type also lends itself to modification. With one set-up and a stock set of pickups it's the perfect 'pop' guitar. With a humbucker and a high action it can be instant Elmore James. A 'hard tail' adaption and lace sensors gives you 'Classic Clapton', a little vibrato abuse and 20 years' practice and you're in Electric Ladyland!

The three guitars built for this book cover classic '50s, '60s and modern 'S' types, and a further modified budget guitar offers humbucker and piezo bridge options. In addition there are DIY 'relic' tips and diagrams for rewiring hot rod switching.

I thought it might also be useful to investigate two successful 'homebuilds' – Brian May's 'Red Special' and Bo Diddley's 'box', as well as examining stringed instrument principles through the simple cigar-box guitar.

So let me guide you through the options and together we'll make the guitars we've dreamed about.

Paul Balmer
Spring 2013

‘A good guitar is one that makes you want to play – you look at the clock and an hour has passed in a moment.’

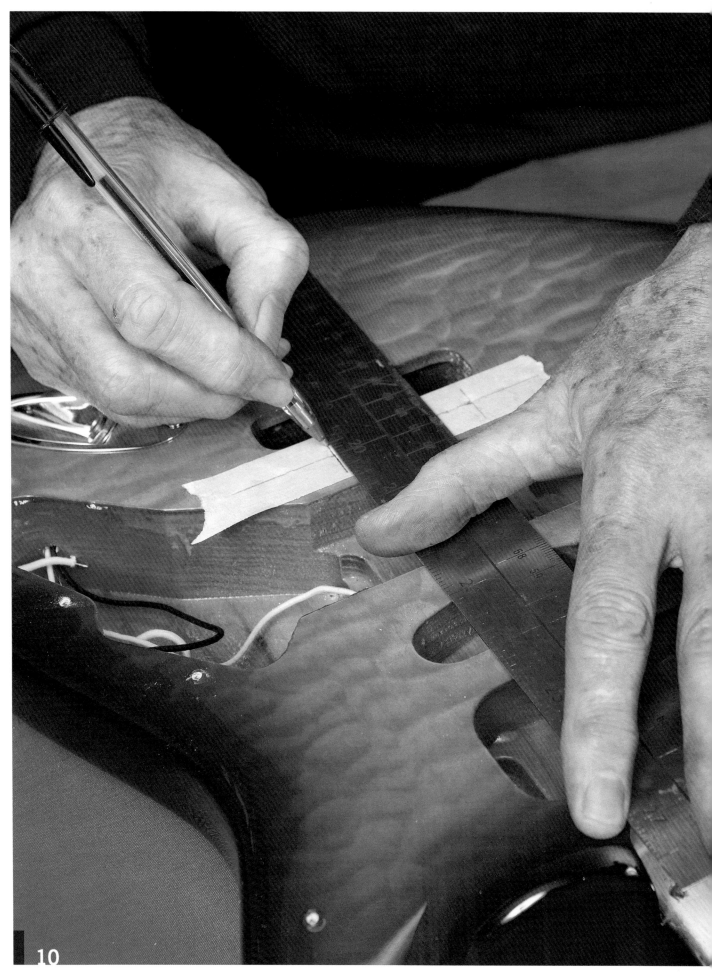

BUILD YOUR OWN ELECTRIC GUITAR

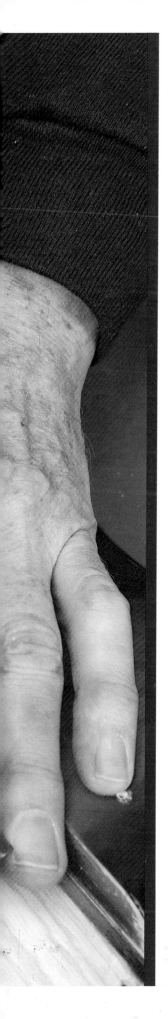

The classic 'S' type

The 'S' type is such a brilliant concept that it's easy to take it for granted. But stepping back and examining the many features that have made it such a winning design explains why, after almost 60 years, they're all still worth incorporating into your own custom guitar.

LEFT Easy assembly.

RIGHT A very modern 'S' type.

11

■ Maple neck and integrated fingerboard

A feature of the original concept was the one-piece 'disposable' neck. Prior to 1920 most guitars were strung with low-tension 'gut' strings, and many early 20th-century guitars have warped necks due to the 'new' strain of metal strings. The 'S' type usually has a relatively accessible adjustable metal truss rod in order to prevent and rectify neck-warping problems. Later 'S' type necks have easier truss rod access at the headstock.

■ Body contours

Early solid body electric guitars had a simple wooden slab body that could dig into your chest on a long session. The 'S' type solution is outrageous, pragmatic, simple and effective.

■ Double cutaways

These enable easy access to the 'dusty end of the fingerboard'. Guitarists would soon exploit the top octave of the guitar, which had been previously difficult to access and largely neglected. This simple innovation radically changed the sound of popular music in the mid-20th century.

Originally the 'S' type featured 21 frets, giving a top C#. This seemingly odd choice reflects the guitar's 'home key' of E, which has C# as its major sixth. Later guitars have an added 22nd fret giving a top D, the flat 7th also in key of E.

■ Body

'S' type bodies are variously made of pine, maple, ash, mahogany, alder, agathis and even occasionally rosewood. Each wood has a subtly different effect on the acoustic sound of the guitar, and this carries over to the amplified sound. The body is not always 'one-piece', and there's an argument for the increased strength of laminates. The classic shape is the perfect synergy of design and use – perfectly balanced and sexy.

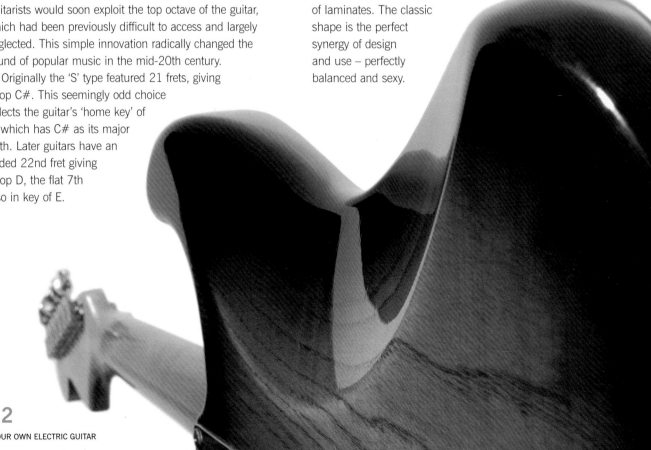

■ Nut

The relatively
narrow nut is
regarded as
an aid to easy
playing in the
first position.

■ Position markers

Traditional Spanish
guitars have no position
marker 'dots', but with
the access to the higher
positions afforded by the
'S' type such visual clues
are very welcome.

■ Tremolo/vibrato

An innovation that changed the sound of popular music. This
isn't the first 'vibrato' device, but is the first that worked without
causing intonation problems. It employs the deceptively simple
mechanics of a balanced fulcrum. The inventor had Hawaiian
and steel guitar sounds in mind, 'subtle vibratos' and glissandi.
The Jimi Hendrix innovations of 'dive bombing' (lowering all
the strings simultaneously) and de-tuning were clearly
inconceivable in 1954. The designer simply opened
a window that players leapt through with enthusiasm.

The misnomer 'Tremolo' has virtually reinvented the word

for two generations of guitarists. It's easy to confuse the notions
of 'vibrato', a note with wavering pitch, with 'tremolo', a rapidly
repeated note (similar to mandolin technique, or as in Francisco
Tarrega's famous study).

British guitarists were amongst the first to truly embrace
the potential of this device. In the early 1960s Hank Marvin
invented a whole playing style built on the subtle portamento
and vibrato potential of Leo Fender's innovation. In the early
21st century Jeff Beck has taken the whole thing a stage
further, inventing a whole new set of techniques.

Access to the vibrato
mechanism is via a rear
plastic panel incorporating
string-threading holes.

It's worth noting that
the tremolo/vibrato arm or
'whammy bar' is supposed
to be held in a suitable
playing position by a tiny
spring, which creates simple
friction pressure on the
base of the arm. This
spring is often lost,
as many players
don't even know
it's supposed to
be there. It's
5/32in size.

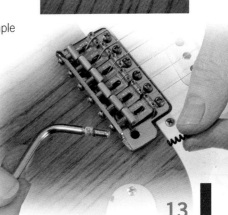

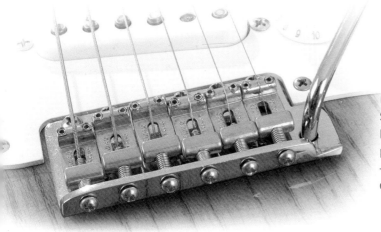

■ **Strap button**

Seems obvious now but many guitarists had previously played seated – you don't really sit down to play an 'S' type.

■ **Micro-adjustable bridge**

The 'S' type set a standard with its introduction of a bridge mechanism that allowed individual adjustment of both the height and length of *each* string. Ironically the precise clarity of the guitar's single coil pickups made this innovation a necessity, and like so many innovations it now seems obvious. The Gibson company were tackling the same challenges with their 'Tune-O-Matic' solution. The 'S' type solution adopts a more blatant 'engineering' approach that was more acceptable on a revolutionary design like the 'S' type than it would be on a contemporary Gibson guitar, where a more 'evolutionary' approach to the development of the electric guitar was adopted. The individual string intonation adjustment was an evolution from work on the significantly titled 'Precision' bass, not the 'T' type guitar, though the 'S' type was the first to actually feature this solution as standard equipment. The bass finally acquired this facility in 1957 and the 'T' type in 1983.

■ **Three-way or five-way pickup selector switch**

Originally the concept was 'one pickup at a time', but combined pickups at positions two and four are now the norm. Both three- and five-way switches are available for ease of use and practical onstage application.

■ **Volume and tone potentiometers**

A simple arrangement developed from 1930s radio circuits. The resistive capacitor circuit usually de-emphasises selected frequencies in the pickup circuit of the middle and neck pickups, though other options are possible.

■ **String tree**

A simple design that improves the engagement of the strings at the guitar nut. This innovation has undergone several redesigns.

■ **Recessed jack socket**

Easier to handle than the edge-fixed socket common on earlier guitars. Neat and effective.

■ Single-row machines

Having the machines on the player's side of the neck in a single accessible row isn't a first, but is convenient and also helps achieve a more stable 'straight' string path.

■ Three pickups

These are a development of pickups made for lap steel guitars. The pickups feature 'harmonic positioning'. The neck pickup is positioned at a point where it will most emphasise the fundamental harmonic, the bridge pickup to most emphasise the higher order harmonics.

■ Pickguard

A combined pickguard and electronics mount means all the guitar's electrics are assembled as a one-piece single-mount component. This sometimes incorporates a metal layer intended to improve electronic screening.

■ Four-bolt neck

A simple and effective design that enables a damaged neck to be replaced. Three-bolt necks are less stable and best avoided.

■ Enclosed machine heads

Enclosed machines were in fact known in the 19th century, but they became more of a necessity in the gritty environment of rock'n'roll. More stable modern tuners are bolted on, and have more precise gearing ratios.

■ Patented headstock

Originating with Stauffer in Germany in the 1850s and featured by Paul Bigsby on his early electric guitars, this design is now legally claimed by a US manufacturer. Though licensed to several other firms, it's certainly wiser to avoid copying this and enjoy being different.

BUILD YOUR OWN ELECTRIC GUITAR

Choosing ideal components

What an opportunity – to custom design *your own* perfect 'S' type! All electric guitarists have some affection for this familiar guitar, but having played a few you may wonder *why* one feels so right while another feels just ordinary. The harder you look the more mysterious it seems to get. I had to make choices for our 'example' guitars, but I will also point out options, where you can make your own decisions. Let's explore the possibilities and strive for some synergy.

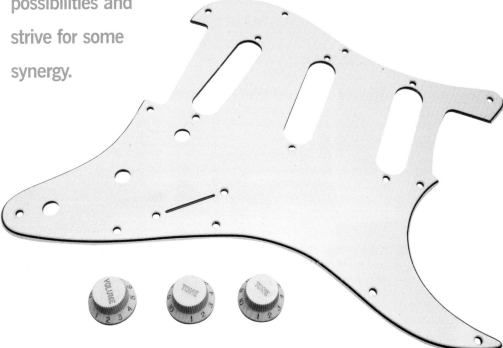

LEFT Fret 'choking' on a 7.25-radius fingerboard.

RIGHT Scratchplate options.

The body

In the beginning the 'S' type was shaped from ash, and the inventors only switched to alder due to grain issues ruining finishes. Good swamp ash smells fantastic – and isn't too heavy, plus if we get the right sample then hopefully grain won't be an issue.

■ Pickup cut-outs

Luthier suppliers Stewart MacDonald and others offer an accurate two-piece shaped ash body with pickup routing ready for a range of pickups, from three single coils to three humbuckers.

Many classic '50s 'S' types were made of more than one piece of timber so we needn't insist on a one-piece body. Some luthiers even argue that a composite body is stronger. The unfinished Stewart MacDonald body has the classic shape and an accurately cut neck pocket (without screw holes), rear trem compartment (with earth cable hole), jack-socket cavity and electrical cut-out. They now also offer classic 'minimal' cut-outs in ash and alder.

1950s pattern

If you're keen on more minimal routing and the classic three single coils pickup arrangement, then at present Allparts and Warmoth are two of many component suppliers offering a licensed alder body cut out in a minimal late 1950s pattern for the pickups – one difference being that these bodies are deeply cut in the control area, which is an advantage if you're thinking of adding modern push-pull pots or other extra electronics.

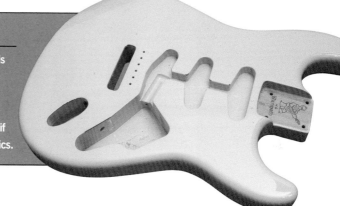

18

■ Wood

Every piece of wood is individual – the width of the grain, the twist in the grain, the density, the water retention, the weight – and all these variables play a part. I've played very light old 'S' types that sound great and very new and sometimes heavy 'S' types that also sound great – but 'different'. Their individuality I interpret as character, and the only recommendation I can give is find something that inspires you to play more, which will improve your playing and will encourage you to play even more – and so it goes on in an upward spiral.

Some luthiers 'tap' solid bodies and listen for the acoustic response, but what are they listening for? Les Paul told me he wanted his guitar bodies to be like a railway sleeper – solid and inert. This leaves the string to vibrate without phase cancellations from resonance. I once owned a 1930s Rickenbacker made from Bakelite; this was solid and inert and the string tone was fabulous, but quiet when unplugged. Plugged in, the Rickenbacker sustained wonderfully. However, a solid wooden guitar that resonates freely when unplugged often sounds good amplified. It's a conundrum.

A resonant piece of wood affects the tone of a note by absorbing some frequencies and reinforcing others in unpredictable ratios. Generally a resonant guitar body tends to have less sustain un-amplified for the simple reason that the energy has been dissipated in making the body vibrate.

Scientific analysis of solid guitar resonance shows simple sine wave-like patterns in the 50Hz–400Hz areas which are made complex by the interaction of different waves at different frequencies. This complexity is naturally exaggerated as we play a range of single notes over a three-and-a-half octave range. *Then* we add a metal bridge attached to a chunk of trem block, and if we're lucky a little magic happens! From an analytical standpoint, if you then play a chord the whole thing gets exponentially more complex. Oh, and then the pickups move, cancelling out some of the string vibration! At higher frequencies the maths disappears into a complex equation currently difficult to fathom.

Soon computer analysis will advance to the point where we *will* be able to put a great 1950s 'S' type under the microscope and say, 'Hey, *this* is what's happening!' However, making it happen *again* with a *different* piece of wood is a whole different challenge (whereas – theoretically – pickups can be scientifically replicated).

I suggest you buy a body from a trusted supplier and spin the wheel – unbiased by measured weight or perceived grain. It's ultimately the synergy of wood, pickups, amp and player that creates a great sound. I remind myself sometimes that if my guitar sounds 'off' it's often a 'software' problem – as in I haven't played enough recently!

Warping and shrinkage

John Diggins, who is the luthier behind this series of books and keeps me on track, recommends keeping any raw timber – whether pre-cut or not – in a warm, dry environment for a few weeks before doing any assembly work. Wood is naturally hydroscopic and therefore absorbs a lot of moisture from the air, which can distort your measurements and lead to annoying post-construction warping and shrinkage. Before doing any finishing work on a wooden neck, always check the neck is 'true' and free from humps, bumps and twists. Any finishing work on a neck that's out of true will necessarily have to be redone – which is a great time waster.

■ Finish

If you're starting from raw wood you can choose your own finish – one of the most personal aspects of *your* guitar. The 'ready-finished' options include this striking flame top currently offered by Stewmac of Ohio. This comes with cut-outs for two humbuckers and a single coil, but could work fine with three single coils or any combination except three humbuckers. The cap is

quilted maple on a swamp ash body with a tough polyester finish (see *Useful contacts* appendix).

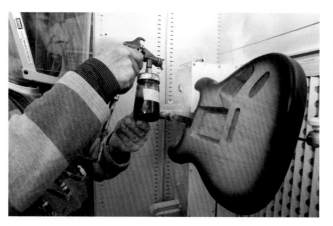

For my favourite choice of ash and two-colour sunburst I'll buy a body and supervise the spraying in a pro paint shop.

Safety first

Finishing a body implies access to a finishing shop and some expertise, as well as an understanding of the many health and safety considerations, so you may want to consider a pre-finished set of components for your first venture.

You *could* even try a DIY job with off-the-shelf spray cans, but it's very hard to create a dust-free environment in your home garage, and paints and solvents can be dangerous to your health if the spray is inhaled. (Please see the safety notes on pages 34–35 before choosing this route.)

Even at a spray shop with an expert doing the work, custom aspects of the guitar can be achieved by choosing a very specific colour and even, say, specifying the shading of the sunburst to bring out the best in the available grain. Doing this in consultation with the spray shop expert can be a very rewarding cooperation.

Nitrocellulose or plastics?

Traditionally the 'S' type is finished in nitrocellulose and theories abound regarding the porous nature of nitro allowing the wood to continue seasoning. Nitro can also be applied very thinly, and both factors may affect sound, but this is very hard to measure scientifically. Hard plastics such as polyester and polyurethane are less porous but more durable – they're also safer to apply. Nitrocellulose is so hazardous as to be banned in California, which presents problems for spray shops.

The neck

Les Paul often espoused the desirability of a rigid neck that didn't dissipate energy. This makes sense. The 'S' type inventors were actually using maple because it was strong and might not need a truss rod.

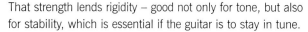

That strength lends rigidity – good not only for tone, but also for stability, which is essential if the guitar is to stay in tune.

In the late '50s a slab of rosewood applied as a fingerboard reinforced that rigidity and stability – possibly the reason why some guitarists believe the slab fingerboard 'S' types are the best.

The Canadian-made Stewmac neck has the 21st-century standard 22 frets and a pre-applied satin polyurethane finish. Other options to consider include these 'C' profile '60s necks and 'boat' profile '50s necks.

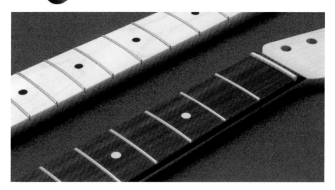

ABOVE Maple or rosewood fingerboard?

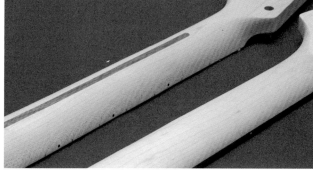

ABOVE Chunky boat neck, or slim '60s?

■ Fingerboards

I prefer maple fingerboards – so does Eric Clapton; others insist rosewood gives a warmer tone. It's down to taste and, again, no two neck woods are identical.

LEFT This rosewood board neck has an off-the-shelf compound radius.

■ Truss rod

Truss rods were first introduced in 1921 and stayed – and that's a darn good thing, as necks bend and you need scope for correction. We must decide if our custom 'S' type is to have authentic butt end adjustment (which is more difficult to adjust) or modern neck end adjustment.

This Warmoth neck has an intriguing and useful side-accessed adjustment on an otherwise vintage-look neck. However, Warmoth advise de-tensioning the strings before adjustment.

■ Headstock

Stauffer/Bigsby shape, or something more radical? This Stewart MacDonald neck leaves you plenty of room for creativity.

Be aware that the holes in this particular neck are cut out for modern bolt-on machines, so you'll need bushings to accommodate traditional Kluson-shaped machines.

■ Frets

The first 'S' types had fairly narrow frets on a fingerboard with a very steep radius as narrow as 7in. Though this suited the playing styles of the 1950s, most current players prefer a flatter board and wider frets. So make a choice informed by playing guitars with a range of characteristics. You could even get a luthier to make you a compound radius – flatter at the body end of the fingerboard as found on very expensive custom guitars such as PRS. This maple neck has a 10in radius and 2.49mm frets, slightly flatter than the modern USA standard, with a lip extension for the extra fret.

■ Nut

Bone or plastic? Tusq or graphite? Fossilised mammoth? Fixed or locking? The choice is yours. You can make your own from a raw bone blank or buy one pre-formed and customise it.

■ These Stewmac bone nuts are pre-slotted and come in different widths and with flat or radiused bases.

■ These Earvana nuts are pre-compensated for very precise intonation. Those shown are for a Gibson, but they're also available for 'S' types.

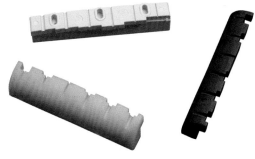

Hardware

Many a potentially good guitar is badly let down by cheap, insubstantial hardware. Don't economise on tuners and bridges, as without tuning stability the guitar will simply drive you insane. Nothing defines an electric guitar sound more than its pickups, so buy the best you can afford.

■ String trees

The original 'washer', seagull wings, or modern trees? As long as they're lubricated they all work. The seagull type is used with and without various spacers for optional heights – whatever gives enough downward pressure at the nut without snagging. Some guitarists like two trees for first and second, and third and fourth strings.

■ Jack socket and plate

The plate needs to be as classy as the original. Just make sure the internal socket itself is the highest possible quality – cheap ones let you down. Mono or stereo? Split the pickups to separate amps? Piezo output on one leg of the stereo? Everything is possible!

■ Machine heads

It's interesting how many players come back to the original Kluson design after having experimented with more sophisticated but heavier variants. The new improved Klusons and Kluson-alikes have a better gearing ratio than the old ones and better internal engineering. There's something very tidy about the originals, but consider the modern options as well – Schaller and Gotoh are up there with Waverley and Grover. Many modern variants lock to the headstock for extra stability.

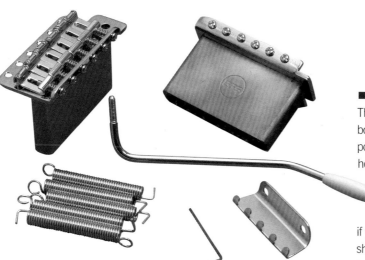

Bridge and trem/vibrato

As with machine heads, many guitarists have experimented with highly sophisticated vibrato units then come back to the original. Like so many aspects of the 'S' type it isn't perfect, but it does work, and perfecting it either dilutes the effect or complicates restringing. Many guitarists have also come back to the original pressed steel saddles and a six-screw fulcrum.

One '70s trend that seems to work is a brass trem block – the extra mass at the string anchor does seem to add extra zing to most 'S' types. Conversely, thin cheap trem blocks sound thin and cheap! Avoid these like cape-wearing synth players. Five springs or three? Blocked off or balanced? Hard to the body? Choices, choices. Experiment until you find what works best for your own playing style.

Sometimes it's worth considering the advantage of a Tremsetter. This will depend on your style of playing but can aid stability without ruining the basic design concept – great if you like to bend strings against open-string 'pedal' notes – see page 128.

Switches

Again, buying the best you can afford makes good sense. There are options offered by 'megaswitches' which particularly come into their own when using four-wire humbuckers and can offer phase, single coil, parallel and series switching options.

Pickups

This area of guitars has entire books devoted to its myriad possibilities. Remember, however, that Jimi Hendrix played stock CBS single coils. Consider stacked humbuckers if you need that extra hum shield. Preserving the classic look is now possible even if you need a non-vintage sound. Consider the pickup types before ordering a pickguard, as cut-outs differ for different types. I suggest you forget all the catalogue hyperbole about sound and try and hear the

options. If that has to be via a website, use good headphones or studio speakers to make an audio assessment. Black or white covers? Staggered poles or flat? Spring suspension or rubber? Alnico 2 or 5? Split coils, parallel or series? Decisions, decisions – again! You may know from experience the sound you're aiming for; if not, you could simply emulate the pickup type of your favourite player. Some luthiers match pickups to body wood types – be aware that a maple cap body with bright single coils will sound exceedingly bright! For more detail on this area see the next chapter.

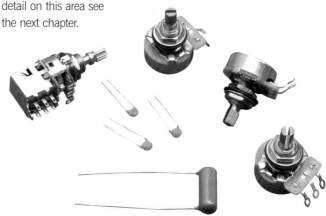

Pots and capacitors

Never economise on potentiometers. The cheap ones become noisy and acquire dead spots very quickly. Also consider the options: linear pots and logarithmic pots both have their fans. Later in this book we'll also explore the advantages and versatility of 'push-pull' pots. Even capacitors have different characteristics, so listen to as many variants as possible, installed in working guitars, before you make your choice.

More hardware

Born of the 1950s, the 'S' type exudes the excitement that the then new plastics offered a designer. The tasteful restraint, a blend of form and function, has survived for 50 years.

■ Pickguards

Pickguards are now available in a vast range of colours and finishes, with cut-outs for single coil, humbucker and mixed arrangements. Preserving the standard three-knob arrangement keeps the classic 'look', but the pots themselves can be multi-function if required. The vintage look is single ply, but screened triple-ply guards are less prone to electronic interference and warping. Black? HSS? More decisions!

If you're unfamiliar with the joys of soldering then pre-loaded pickguards like this Alumitone from Don Lace offer a pre-wired solution.

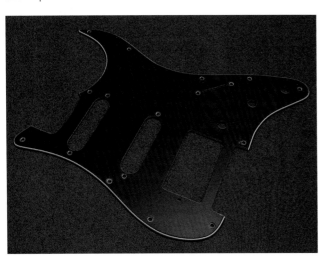

■ Knobs

Original early '50s types are hard to find but the classic 'flying saucer' is available in a range of colours. You could, of course, go for something entirely different if the vintage look isn't your thing.

Aesthetics

If you are drawn to the 'relic' look then many manufactures now offer aged parts – these can be cream or 'mint', to ape the different decay characteristics of early plastics, or pre-tarnished for metal. If you want you can DIY distress new-look components. See the later section on 'A little light relic work' (page 130) for more on this.

Trem arm tip – aged, white or redundant?

■ Trem cover

The trem cover is available with a variety of string holes, and the more modern larger access can save a bit of fiddly string-changing. Single ply or triple ply? Aged, white or redundant?

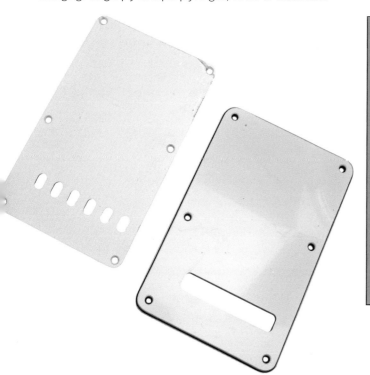

■ Neckplate, strap buttons and screws

It's easy to overlook these small but important parts. Go for a 'look' – chrome or nickel? New or aged? Is it worth installing a straplock system from the start – especially if the guitar's going to be heavily gigged?

■ Electrical wire

I use 'vintage' push-back cloth-covered wire for ease of use and a cool look!

Choices

The appendices include a checklist (page 154) so that you can be sure you have everything you need before you start assembling your guitar (it can be frustrating waiting for missing parts to arrive!), but as we go through the assembly processes in this book I'll explain my own parts choices and the reasons I made them – you can then, of course, choose to differ! The end results are discussed in detail in Outcomes, on page 138.

Matching pickguards & pickups

One of the useful design features of the 'S' type guitar is its 'loaded' pickguard capability – designed for ease of production assembly, all the electronics apart from the jack socket are self-contained. This presents ease of access for maintenance and scope for versatility in the pickup department.

A huge range of colour and texture finishes is available as well as white, black, 'shell' and vintage-aged 'mint' and cream.

This 'pre-loaded' Lace pickguard offers three unusual Alumitone aluminium pickups, with only three solder points to complete the assembly. Alumitones are, as their name suggests, made predominantly of aluminium, so there's even less interference with string-sensing magnetic fields.

However, it's worth buying a pre-cut guard with your required pickup slots, the most common being this familiar white, three single-coil three-ply arrangement.

Another common arrangement offers 'HSS' or humbucker at the bridge and two single coils.

Two humbuckers and two P90s cut-outs are also available, if harder to locate, and some manufacturers will offer custom cutting for unusual pickup configurations.

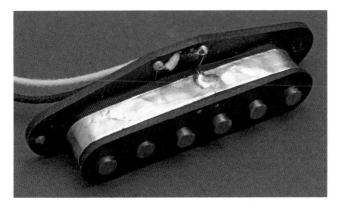

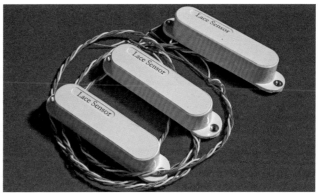

Even if you're sticking to a three single-coil look you have an enormous choice of options, from 'vintage spec' pickups such as the Stewmac 'Golden Age' for the sound of '54. These are wax-potted with AWG42 coil windings and Alnico 5 staggered pole pieces.

Each pickup has a copper shield surrounding the coil, a modern feature for 50/60-cycle hum suppression not found on vintage pickups.

To play 'naked', vintage-style, you could simply snip the small jumper wire that connects the foil to the pickup's ground lug. These pickups are supplied with traditional rubber grommet suspension and black and white covers. This is the spec:

#5420 neck polarity south 6.0K
#5421 middle polarity north 6.0K
#5422 bridge polarity south 6.4K

The 'Golden Age' range includes an overwound bridge or neck pickup #5423 with polarity south and resistance 7.6K.

This is similar to that offered by branded Alnico 5 'Texas Specials'. These are associated with the sound of Stevie Ray Vaughan and installed on his custom shop guitar.

Standard Lace sensors offer less magnetic interference with the string excursion by using a very focused approach to the magnetic field. These were used for many years by Eric Clapton and Pete Townshend.

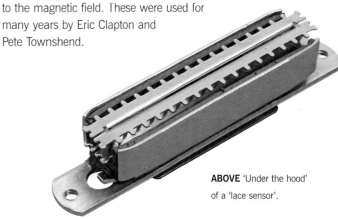

ABOVE 'Under the hood' of a 'lace sensor'.

Another option is pre-harnessed Kinman pickups, which again require little soldering if any. Kinman also offer 'noiseless' single coils which, in an increasingly busy ether, may be a good choice. Their design rejects RF interference and 50/60-cycle mains hum. These are 'Woodstocks' without the noise (which is an interesting concept).

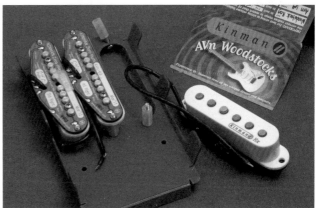

RIGHT A 'Golden Age' humbucker.

Principally for their distinct tone rather than any noise rejection, many 'S' type players have opted for the humbucker option in either the neck or bridge position or both. This example is also from the 'Golden Age' range.

As with many modern humbuckers this one combines vintage tone with modern versatile four-wire circuitry. The advantage of the four-wire is that one pickup can offer many sounds from traditional series wiring to parallel, coil-tapped, single coil, and 'out of phase'. In conjunction with a megaswitch all these options can be readily available when installed on the guitar.

I would strongly suggest you try a classic PAF-style humbucker initially, as these produce enough output without getting overly muddy – a tendency with some overwound types. Seymour Duncan 'Jazz' humbuckers are a good, modern balanced option. Seymour also offers an interesting humbucker which is made from two genuine single coils – this works very well when used in combination with other single coils on the same guitar.

All the hardware for this type of guitar is available gold-plated for very little more money, so you may want to consider a little 'bling' – as on these Ibanez humbuckers with gold covers.

Before purchasing a pickguard decide if you're having an exterior cover on the humbucker or not, as this will affect the cut-out size. It's not easy to resize the plastics neatly without specialist tools. Generally removing the cover brings out slightly more high frequencies compared to covered pickups, which sound a little more mellow due to the cover soaking up some stray capacitance; it's all a matter of taste.

■ **Balanced pickup outputs**

Once you've decided your pickup configuration you can choose from a bewildering range of individual pickup manufacturers. The key thing here is balance. It can be very disconcerting on stage if the guitar output fluctuates dramatically when selecting different positions with your five-way switch. Many manufactures offer custom sets intended to balance and complement, as well as a pre-wired 'out of phase' middle pickup that offers the benefit of humbucking cancellation effects in positions two and four.

Some manufacturers, including Trevor Wilkinson, also offer special single-coil pickups designed to balance with a humbucker in an HSS (humbucker/single coil/single coil) arrangement. This is definitely worth considering early as you design your ideal guitar, as pickups are expensive components to replace later.

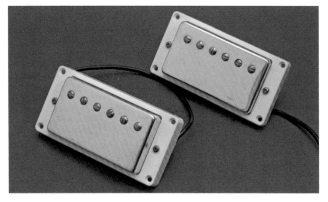

Reclaimed, recycled and licensed components

One possibility presented by the component nature of the 'S' type is the reuse of recycled parts from earlier and discarded instruments. It's worth exploring the Internet, yard sales and even local second-hand stores for damaged instruments with any intact parts. An American 'S' type with a broken neck may be the perfect economy source for some excellent electrics. Equally, a badly damaged body might provide the opportunity for a refurbishment and custom finish.

Older parts often have a patina and mojo not found on new parts, and can often be a bargain – as long as they're working well.

Things to avoid

- Badly warped or worn necks, frets and fingerboards – these are labour intensive to repair and will cost more than buying them new.

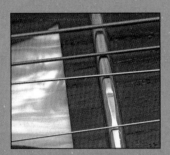

- Old and rusty machine heads – these will be a tuning nightmare. Enclosed Kluson types are often rusty internally after 50 years so the damage is less apparent.

- Rusted steel saddles with worn screws and Allen bolts are more trouble than they're worth.

- Damaged trem fulcrums – difficult and expensive to repair. Examine the bearing edges for indentations and distortions; they should be even and have the correct bevel.

- Cheap lightweight trem blocks, which are detrimental to tone and stability.

- Worn 'noisy' pots and switches – they'll let you down on stage. Particularly avoid cheap economy PCB-type switches.

Discarded guitars can nevertheless be a great source for solid peripherals such as string trees, strap locks, solid steel trem blocks, jack socket retainers and trem covers. Be aware, however, of the different and incompatible screw location patterns on some guitars' pickguards, and also incompatible threads on some trem arms.

Upgrading or repairing an existing guitar with licensed parts

Several manufacturers, including Warmoth, now have licensing agreements with the US 'S' type originators. Consequently authentic parts can be obtained for repairs and upgrades, which will maintain the value of such instruments without infringing on design copyrights. Be aware, however, that these parts are intended purely for installation on authentic, licensed instruments, and there may be patent issues to consider, especially regarding patented headstock designs.

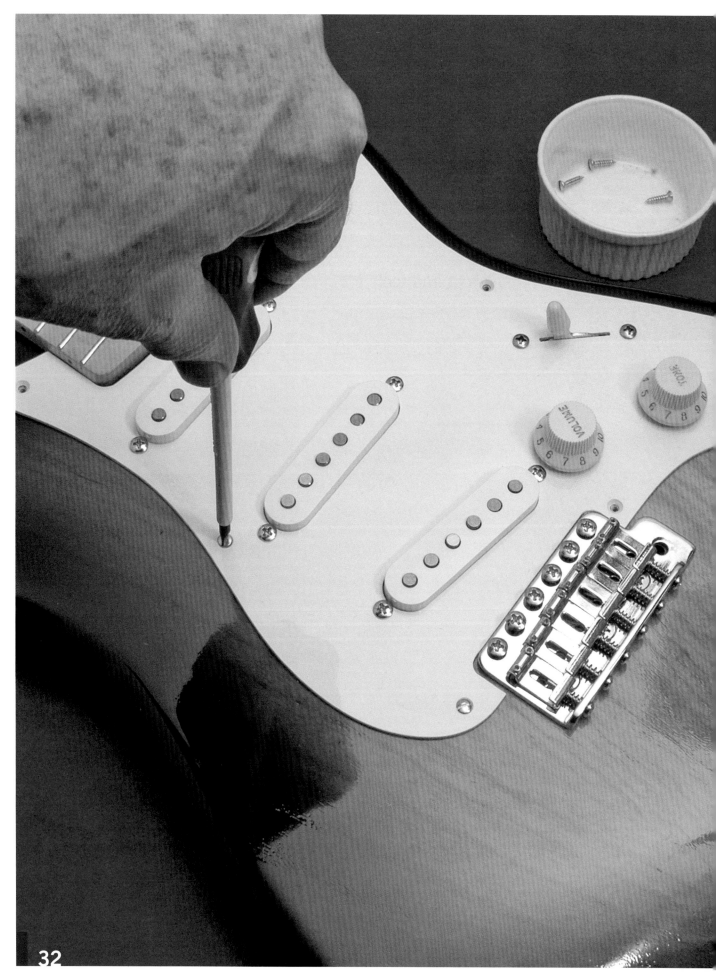

Getting started

Ideally, you should try to allocate a dedicated space in your home for this project. You can then have all the components and required tools easily to hand. It also means you can leave a part-assembled guitar safely aside while you get on with the many daily demands we all face.

Try and avoid any artificial pressure to finish. Award yourself the luxury of thinking time, which is often missing from an assembly line. Try to make you guitar considered and uncompromised and, above all, be safe.

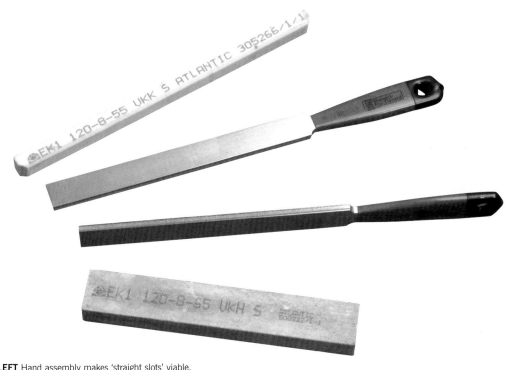

LEFT Hand assembly makes 'straight slots' viable.

RIGHT Hand tools are satisfying to use and allow thinking time.

Safety first

The electric guitar is no more dangerous to work on,
or perform with, than any other DIY project. However,
there are some hazards of which you should be aware.

Electric shock

You may be using power tools and soldering irons, so the usual precautions apply. A circuit breaker can slow you down a bit but it may save your life! Consider using an earth leakage trip or similar circuit breaker in any situation where you have no control or knowledge of the mains power.

You'll be testing your components using an amplifier. Sadly many guitar players have either been killed or badly burned through accidental exposure to mains current. Though the UK's adoption of 240V may seem to present a greater risk than the USA's 110V, it's actually the amperes that are the killer, not the volts! Amperes are the measure of current, and high currents are the ones to avoid.

Guitar amplifiers run happily on domestic supplies at relatively low current ratings, so the situation of one guitarist one amp is a pretty safe scenario, especially if we observe a few precautions:

■ Always ensure a good earth or ground connection.
  This allows a safe path to earth for any stray current, which always flows along the easiest path. The earth or ground offers a quicker route to earth than through you and therein lies its safety potential.
■ Never replace fuses with the wrong value, eg a 5-amp fuse in a 3-amp socket. Fuses are there to protect us and our equipment from power surges. A higher value means less protection. Never replace a fuse with a bodge such as silver foil or similar. This offers no protection at all.
■ Maintain your mains leads. Check them regularly for damage and strained wires. If fitted the earth wire must be in place.
■ Never operate an amplifier with the safety cover removed, especially valve amplifiers known for their HT circuits.
■ Never put drinks on or near amplifiers.
■ Never touch a stage lighting circuit or lamp. Apart from mains electricity issues they're often also dangerously hot. Leave stage lamps to qualified electricians.

If playing at a live gig beware in addition of

■ Multi amp/multi PA scenarios that aren't professionally administered. Professional PA and lighting supervisors are very safety-conscious and trained in health and safety to a legal minimum requirement. The danger comes with 'semi pro' and amateur rigs which aren't closely scrutinised. If you're in any doubt don't plug in until you've talked to the on-site supervisor and feel you can trust his assurances.
■ Unknown stage situations, especially those which feature big lighting rigs. This is easily said but hard to adhere to. Even the most modest gigs nowadays have quite sophisticated lights and sound. The crucial issue is that all the audio equipment is connected to the same PHASE. Danger particularly arises when microphones are connected to one PHASE and guitars and instruments to another. An instrumentalist/vocalist could find himself as the 'bridge' between 30 amps of current! If in any doubt be rude and ask.

Hearing damage

Leo Fender's first guitar amp knocked out a feverish 4W of audio; but by the early '60s Paul McCartney had a T60. By 1964 The Beatles had the first 100W VOX amps, specifically made to cope with concerts in vast football stadiums and the noise of immense screaming crowds.

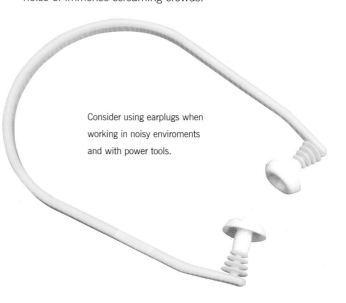

Consider using earplugs when working in noisy enviroments and with power tools.

Chemical hazards

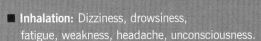

Paints and solvents

Traditionally electric guitars were painted with nitrocellulose lacquer and this practice continues on many, especially 'vintage' reissues. Nitrocellulose lacquers produce a very hard yet flexible, durable finish that can be polished to a high gloss. The drawbacks of these lacquers include the hazardous nature of the solvent, which is flammable, volatile and toxic. The dangers inherent in the inhalation of spray paints are serious enough to be covered by legal statutes in the USA, UK and Europe.

Symptoms

- **Acute and chronic ingestion:** Large doses may cause nausea, narcosis, weakness, drowsiness and unconsciousness.
- **Inhalation:** Irritation to nose and throat. At high concentrations, same effects as ingestion.
- **Skin:** Cracking of skin, dermatitis, and secondary infections.
- **Eyes:** Irritation.
- **Symptoms of overexposure:** Repeated skin contact may cause dermatitis, while the skin defatting properties of this material may aggravate an existing dermatitis.
  (Source: Material Safety Data Sheet.)

Polyurethane hazards

Vapours may accumulate in inadequately ventilated/confined areas, and may form explosive mixtures with air. Vapours may travel long distances and flashback may occur. Closed containers may explode when exposed to extreme heat.

Symptoms

- **Ingestion:** May be similar to inhalation symptoms – drowsiness, dizziness, nausea, irritation of digestive tract, depression, aspiration hazard.

- **Inhalation:** Dizziness, drowsiness, fatigue, weakness, headache, unconsciousness.
- **Skin:** Drying, cracking, dermatitis.
- **Eyes:** Burning, tearing, reddening. Possible transient corneal injury or swelling of conjunctiva.
  (Source: Carbon Black Carcinogen by IARC, Symptoms of Overexposure.)

Recommended precautions

Always wear goggles/full face shield and other protective equipment. Avoid skin contact by wearing protective clothing. Take a shower and bathe your eyes after exposure. Wash contaminated clothing thoroughly before reusing it. … So, with all this in mind, remember that the addresses of recommended guitar repair men and spray shops can be found in your local *Yellow Pages*.

You must take extreme precautions, particularly to avoid inhalation of the dangerous mist created by the spray process. A passive mask available from DIY stores will only offer the most minimal protection. If in any doubt consult the paint manufacturer for detailed precautions specific to the paint type you've chosen.

By 1970 100W was the norm for a guitar 'head' in a small club and the first 10,000W PA systems had rocked Woodstock.

Pete Townshend of The Who first complained of the hearing impairment tinnitus in the mid-'70s and for many years refused to tour with a band as his hearing worsened.

The key to saving your hearing is 'dose' figures. Research has shown that you risk damage if exposed to sound 'dose' levels of 90dB or above for extended periods. Health and safety limits for recording studios now recommend no more than 90dBA

('A' standing for average) per eight-hour day, these levels to be reduced dramatically if the period is longer or the dbA higher.

Transient peaks, as in those produced by a loud snare drum or hi-hat, can easily push levels beyond these figures. Be careful where you stand in relation to drums and amplifiers – a small movement can effect a dramatic change in transient sound level. Don't be afraid to ask about peak and average levels. Your ears are your greatest asset as a musician, so don't be embarrassed into thinking you can't question sound levels.

Tools and working facilities

Much of the assembly and fitting we'll be doing can be done using regular domestic workshop tools. However, a few specialist luthiers' tools can often make jobs easier and safer.

Workshop tools

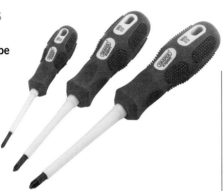

■ Set of Phillips-type screwdrivers, sizes '0', '1' and '2'

It may seem a small point, but I recommend using the correct size and type of screwdriver. Many valuable guitars have survived 30 years on the road but often have a selection of odd screws and 'stripped' screw heads. These look unsightly, slow you down and make the simplest job a chore. The correct 'point' size will reduce screw stripping and is also less likely to skate across your prized paintwork.

- Use size '0' for some Kluson-type machine heads and truss rod shields.
- Use size '1' for pickguard, rear access covers, jack socket, some machine-head screws and strap buttons.
- Use size '2' for neck bolts.

A screwdriver with interchangeable heads is an alternative option. However, you'll often need several heads at the same time, which means a lot of changing around. This option is nevertheless useful on the road, when a compact toolkit is more practical.

Sometimes an electric screwdriver can take the strain out of repetitive tasks. However, be sure to protect the guitar as the screwdriver 'torques out'. Never use one on plastic parts, as old plastics become brittle and easily crack under sudden pressure. With a Zap-It attachment an electric screwdriver can also double as a string winder.

■ Set of car feeler gauges (.002–.025in) (0.05–1mm)

These are used for assessing and setting the string action height.

■ 6in (150mm) ruler with 1/32in and 1/64in (0.5mm) increments

Also used for setting and assessing the string action.

■ Set of digital callipers

Useful for so many measurements.

■ A fret rocker

Brilliant for identifying proud frets.

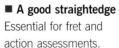

■ A good straightedge

Essential for fret and action assessments.

■ A 'string spacing' rule

The easiest way to assign string slots in the nut.

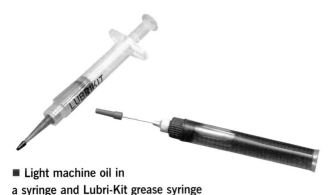

■ Light machine oil in a syringe and Lubri-Kit grease syringe
These can also be used for accurately and sparingly lubricating the saddle contacts, trem and some tuners.

■ Large straight-slot screwdriver
For some truss rods.

■ A set of Allen keys
For saddle and some truss rod adjustments.

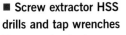

■ Screw extractor HSS drills and tap wrenches
For removing broken screws.

✎ Tech Tip

When working on brittle plastics consider using a fixed torque screwdriver – adjusted to avoid the kind of damage seen on many old guitars. Once set, these screwdrivers cannot over-tighten. Angled drivers are also useful for 'awkward to reach' spots.

Henry Phillips

Have you ever wondered why most guitar manufacturers switched to Phillips-type screws?

In the 1950s many fledgling companies were taking lessons from the streamlined assembly process at Henry Ford's car lines in Detroit. For these, Henry Phillips (1890–1958) had developed the cross-head screw. In 1936 The American Screw Co persuaded General Motors to use the Phillips-head screw in manufacturing Cadillacs, and by 1940 virtually every American automaker had switched to Phillips screws.

This new screw worked well with ratchet and electric screwdrivers, had greater torque, was self-centring, and didn't slip from the slot so easily, avoiding damage to the valuable paintjob. The speed with which Phillips screws can be used was crucial to the auto assembly line. In addition, Phillips screws are almost impossible to over-screw, which was very important.

However, cam-out or torque-out makes tightly driven Phillips screws fiendishly hard to remove and often damages the screw, the driver, and anything else a suddenly loose driver happens to hit. And whereas a coin or a piece of scrap metal can often be used to loosen a slot screw, nothing takes the place of a Phillips screwdriver. A flat-bladed driver or even a wrong-size Phillips just makes cam-out worse.

Beware: Phillips screwdrivers should not be used with Pozidrive screws (and vice versa). They are subtly different and when mixed they tend to ride out of the slot as well as rounding the corners of both the tool and screw recess.

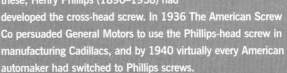

■ Portable suction fixing vice
This ingenious device is terrific if you have no suitable permanent workbench. Ideal for nut filing.

Specialist tools

■ Set of gauged nut files
These will make it a lot easier to set the nut up correctly.

■ Nut seating file
Will ensure a good surface for the nut: better contact = better tone. This 1/8in size is perfect for many 'S' types. A needle file of the correct width may work, so long as the edges are non-abrasive and don't inadvertently alter the 'nut' edge of the slot, as this will affect the intonation.

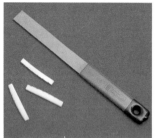

■ Set of accurate radius gauges
These make setting the nut and saddle radii a lot easier.

■ Nut crowning files and diamond stones
Make fret adjustment a lot easier.

■ Nut jig
Takes most of the guesswork out of nut shaping and radius setting.

■ Fret erasers
These gentle and malleable abrasives are graded for brilliant fret finishing – they can also be used with fret guards to avoid damaging maple fingerboards.

■ Electronic tuner
An electronic tuner with a jack socket as opposed to an internal microphone will make short work of adjusting the intonation of individual string lengths. The strobe type are brilliant for intonation setting.

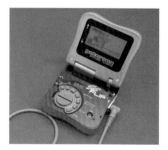

■ Wire cutters
Useful for cutting strings to length. Overlong strings at the headstock are a safety hazard and tear up your gig bag.

■ Polish and cloth
A soft duster for the body and the back of the neck, and a lint-free cotton cloth for strings and fingerboard. Proprietary guitar polishes differ from household furniture polishes, which often contain silicone. The wax used in guitar polish is emulsified to avoid any sticky residue, especially under the heat generated by stage lighting.

Working environment

Most of our assembly can be safely carried out with the guitar resting on a normal kitchen table or on a Workmate-type DIY bench, suitably padded. The work shown in the photographs for this book was 80% done at home on a Draper Workmate. However, see page 35 for precautions regarding the inhalation of cellulose etc. Outside the guitar case environment, a small 1m square of carpet sample Blue-Tacked to a workbench can avoid a lot of inadvertent damage to guitar paintwork.
NB: All the guitar techs and luthiers consulted for this book seemed to have their own ingenious home-made tools for some very specific jobs.

■ Soldering iron

This should be at least 25W with a penlight tip. An iron is essential when replacing worn-out volume pots and three-way switches etc. It's worth investing in a stand with a sponge cleaner attached (Draper components 23554 or similar). A crocodile clip multi-arm is also useful for holding small components in place.

■ Torch-equipped tweezers

For rescuing dropped screws from awkward cavities and removing hot wires during soldering. The built-in torch is very handy when screws drop inside control cavities.

■ A tube of solder

Multicore-type non acid resin.

■ A solder syringe

Makes light work of drawing old solder from previous electrical joints.

■ A small penlite torch

Useful for closer examination of details.

Useful accessories

- ■ Silicone or graphite locksmiths' nut lubricant.
- ■ Matchsticks or cocktail sticks for lubrication application and 'rawlplugging' loose screws.
- ■ Pipe cleaners and cotton buds for cleaning awkward spots; an old electric toothbrush can also be useful.
- ■ An electronic multimeter for testing pickup circuits.
- ■ A set of socket spanners is useful for removing and tightening pot nuts, jack sockets and some machine heads.
- ■ Many guitar nuts can be handled by this single handy Cruztools gizmo (above).
- ■ Loctite or similar multi-purpose superglue.
- ■ Craft knife for nut work.
- ■ Thread gauges, useful for checking for correct threads on replacement screws etc.
- ■ Rubber hammer, safer in many situations on valuable instruments.
- ■ Wire stripper.
- ■ Lemon oil for rosewood fingerboards.
- ■ Spare jack socket, 250K pot, knobs and pickup switch.
- ■ Dental abrasives and/or abrasive cord for fine-tuning a nut slot.

Consider also having a set of bench drawers and tidies for all those often misplaced odds and sods that are essential for guitar maintenance and DIY.

✎ Tech Tip

The worst-case scenario with soldering is melting the plastic on interior wires – so be quick! But also keep the components steady: a wire moved while solder is setting may cause a 'dry joint' and poor conductivity.

John Diggins – Luthier

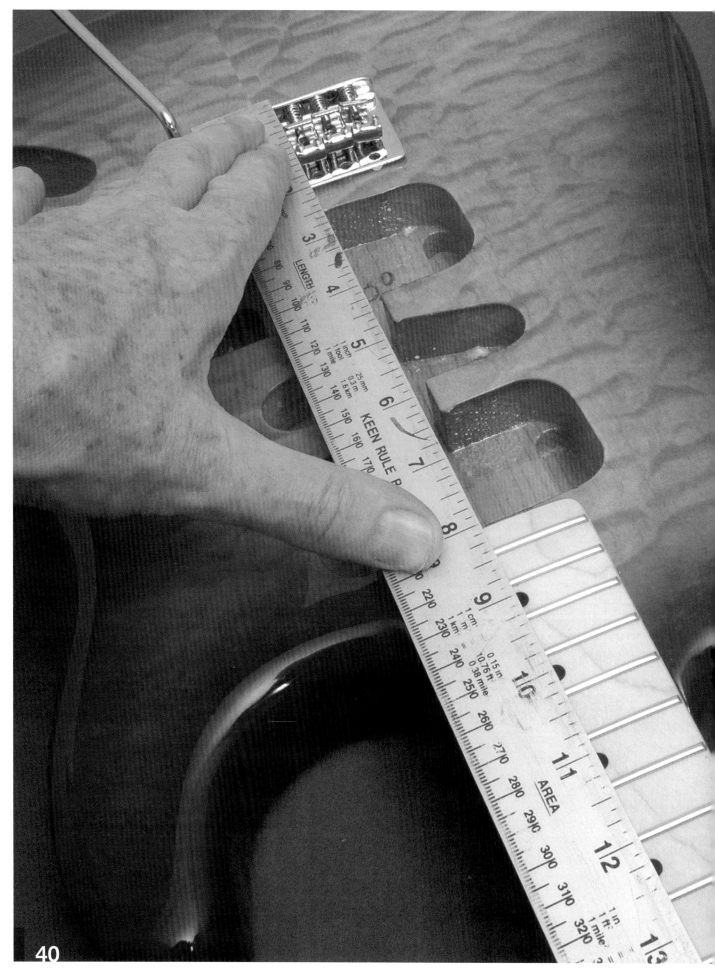

BUILD YOUR OWN ELECTRIC GUITAR

Assembly and fitting 1: pre-finished components

So, we've chosen all the great components we'll need, and sorted out our tools. It's time to get stuck in! But take your time, and don't compromise, as this is your special guitar. If in doubt, leave it out. If you're not sure, check! Many great projects are spoiled by haste and the urge to just get finished. I suggest you enjoy the process itself, and occasionally step back for a day or so and consider the best way to approach the next stage. Whatever the dilemma, you may find a better solution if you simply think about if for a while.

If you're starting from an unfinished body and neck then you'll need to refer to page 78.

Not everybody has access to a finishing shop so I'm going to start by suggesting the easiest route to a custom guitar: assembling and 'fitting' preformed components or substituting better components to an existing instrument – which isn't as easy as I had imagined

LEFT Checking neck and bridge alignment.

Fitting a bridge with integral trem and aligning the neck

It's worth fitting the bridge/trem unit when attaching the neck, as the bridge height and centring will provide a useful reference point for the neck alignment. The neck fitting and bridge positioning are necessarily interrelated, as their relative positions are critical to the guitar's intonation and set-up.

Here I'm fitting a 'vintage'-type GFS brass block trem to our maple cap guitar body (see page 20). I can't recommend the brass block enough, as it improves the acoustic string sustain on any 'S' type.

1 Place the neck in the neck socket and ensure it's sitting correctly. Sometimes the neck is a little over-tight in the socket due to the extra thickness of the finish. The best tactic here is to leave the neck itself 'as is' and carefully adjust the socket. Be aware that any drastic adjustments here will affect the neck angle, so go gently, and ensure all adjustments are flush and 'square'.

All that's required in this specific case is gentle abrasion over the socket edges where the lacquer overlaps. This is done with a little abrasive paper attached to a 'square' batten. Using only gentle 'in' strokes avoids damage to the overlapping lacquer. The Titania chiropodist's file (above right) has the perfect radius for getting into the rounded corners of the pocket.

Aim for a good snug fit for the best 'wood to wood' contact.

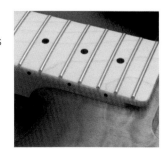

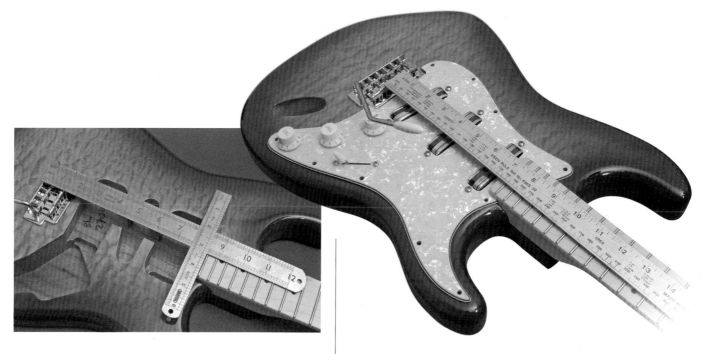

2 Having adjusted the neck pocket, check that the centre of the neck aligns with the centre of the bridge, ensuring that the bridge isn't touching either side of the bridge socket.

■ I've loosely glued a ⅟₁₆in spacer (a child's lolly stick) behind and to one side of the trem block, to ensure some scope for its eventual 'free' pivot. This is just a guide for getting the screw holes in the right place and naturally these will be removed before final fitting.

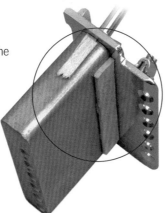

■ Take care that the lolly sticks don't overlap too much at the sides as this can skew your measurements. Assuming the position markers on the neck are correctly aligned (check!), then these make a good guide for checking the neck centring.

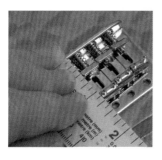

Note the ruler meets the saddles dead centre between the set of six!

3 Roughly place the pickguard to check for any snagging at the trem or neck pocket. Don't worry over any slight chafing, as the pickguard can be trimmed if necessary.

4 Then check the measurement from nut to 12th fret, which should be 12¾in, and from 12th fret to saddles, which should also be 12¾in, with room for adjustment at the saddles.

5 With a bradawl, mark the screw hole positions for the six No '6' bridge screws.

6 Then pilot these with a small hand drill – you'll need a ³⁄₃₂in bit.

7 The screws should now go into the hard timber easily enough. I like to put the bridge fulcrum bearing on the two outer screws only, and leave the centre four relatively loose – this pattern is now common on newer 'S' types. See page 95 for more set-up details.

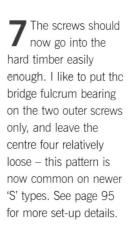

Rear trem unit

The rear trem unit (see page 25) needs to be fitted to give the bridge its proper position – which will eventually be under tension from the string counterbalancing springs. Try to examine an existing 'S' type to further understand this arrangement.

1 Solder the earth or 'ground' wire to the spring retaining claw – you may need to abrade the claw and tin this with a little solder to get a good connection. Some claws, like this one, have a cable hook.

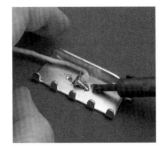

2 Poke the wire through to the pickup cavity.

3 Attach the spring retaining claw. Be sure to position the claw low enough in the cavity as otherwise there's a danger of the trem springs eventually snagging on the rear cover. In a typical 120mm trem cavity, 15mm allowance on the screw protrusion from the timber should get you in the ballpark for a balanced floating trem. In practical terms, working in ash or alder you'll need to pilot these screw holes substantially or the usual 36mm wood screws will be very difficult to move for trem adjustment. Lubricate the screws with a little candle wax.

4 Fit the trem springs. Three springs are usually adequate for 009 or 010 gauge strings. Parallel and fan springing both work, though parallel arrangements are less likely to cause spring distortions and inconsistencies.

Trem cover

You probably want to leave this off until the guitar is fully set up. They vary in detail, but fixing is the same for all. Here I've matched the rear cover to the fancy Lace pickguard.

1 Mark up the screw positions with a sharp bradawl, ensuring the string holes in the trem block line up with those on the cover – otherwise string changing will be difficult.

2 Pilot the holes and fix with six No '4' ½in raised countersunk screws.

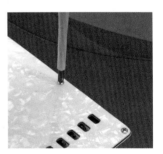

Trem or hard tail set-up?

Even if you prefer not to use a trem, I strongly suggest you install a trem and then block it off, as the sound of the 'S' type is certainly influenced by the trem block and spring assembly. See page 126 for details of a secure 'block off' as used by Eric Clapton and others.

⚡ Tech Tip

Never use cheap screws for guitar assembly: they break, the heads distort, and they rust – it's a false economy you'll regret. Buy high-quality chromed screws of the correct size and Phillips spec. Pozidrivs are a suitable alternative where they're unseen, but don't mix up the drivers – they're incompatible.

John Diggins – Luthier

Bolting the neck

Though often referred to as 'bolting', the usual neck fixing on an 'S' type involves using four 45mm wood screws, free-mounted in pre-drilled neck holes and then secured to the body. The simple neckplate is the best way of evening the distribution of torque on the screws and protecting the body wood.

1 Carefully align the neck and bridge as described in the previous section. Then mark the screw holes with a bradawl.

2 Pilot the body holes with a 2mm drill set with a marker tape to a depth of 12mm.

3 Lubricate the screw threads with a little candle wax. These 'floating' candles are the ideal shape!

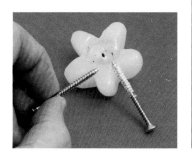

4 Incorporating the neck plate, fix two diagonal screws. Then re-check the neck/bridge alignment with a straight edge. Fixing the other two screws later offers some degree of adjustment potential.

5 Fix the remaining two screws with any slight adjustment required in the neck orientation, which should line up perfectly with the bridge.

■ The chances are that some fine tweaking of the truss rod and neck angle will be required eventually. See page 90.

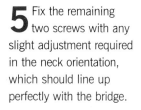

Checking the initial neck alignment

Before getting too carried away with the full assembly I'm going to suggest we fit a couple of tuners and roughly place a temporary nut (you don't need precise nut slots yet) to check that the neck pitch and angle are workable.

3 A socket spanner/wrench avoids damage to the guitar when tightening the bushings. Don't overtighten these, as the shallow thread on the bushing will shear! Add the sixth string tuner.

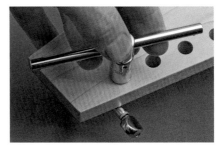

4 Align the tuners with a protractor or square as a guide, and add the fixing screws to the rear. The screws will require a tiny pilot hole drilled in the hard maple and then a No 'O' Phillips driver.

As this is intended to be a 'modern' working guitar I'm going to fit locking bolt-on tuners for more stability – these are JHS lightweight 'minis' from renowned guitar-maker Trevor Wilkinson; these are light enough to avoid making the guitar 'neck-heavy'.

1 Insert the tuner for the first string from the back and add the washer.

2 Add the locking bushing and thread on to the tuner.

5 Fit the two strings and check their alignment with the sides of the neck and the saddle centres. These strings are square to the frets for good intonation, square to the saddles, and in a good position for the pickups.

6 If the strings are running slightly out of true or misaligned to the saddle centres, you need to adjust the bridge or neck to correct this or the guitar won't tune-up.

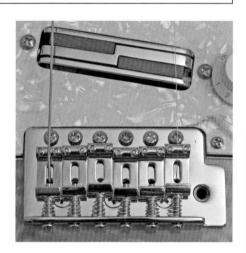

7 If the outer strings do line up correctly, fit the other four tuners and proceed. A ruler placed along the back of the tuner housings ensures the tuner row is neatly aligned before screwing into position.

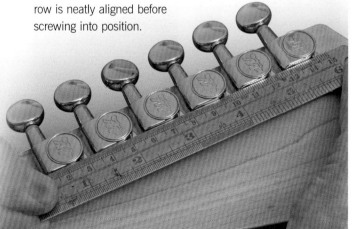

Pickguard fit

It's a good idea to check if the pickguard is clear of the bridge movement at this point.

1 If the plastic guard is chafing slightly on the bridge, as here, then a little gentle filing needs to be done. I'm going to mark for a little to come off both edges – a felt-tip pen mark is easily removed from the protective plastic coating.

2 A flat file achieved the initial trim, then a rat tail file fitting the curvature of the corners nicely was used for shaping.

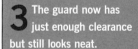

3 The guard now has just enough clearance but still looks neat.

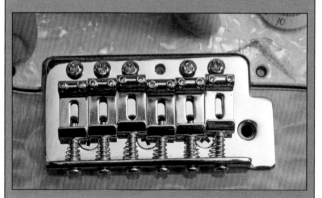

Initial set-up

With the tuners in place we can string the guitar and assess the basic alignment of the bridge, trem, neck and nut. I feel it's important to get all of this working as a guitar before dealing with electrics and ancillary bits and pieces. Good electric guitars usually sound and function well acoustically, albeit quietly.

Balancing the trem

1 Tune the guitar acoustically to A440, using an electronic tuner, tuning fork or another guitar as a reference pitch.

2 In a normal 'floating trem' arrangement with the strings at pitch the trem should sit about ⅛in off the guitar body. You can use the trem cover as a guide – it should slip under the back edge of the bridge.

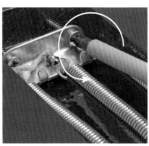

3 If the bridge is too high tighten the trem retaining screws.

4 If it's too low, loosen the trem screws. Re-tension the strings to pitch and recheck until a suitable height is established.

3 With the correct Allen wrench, set the sixth string to a workable height – not too much fret buzz etc.

Setting the bridge saddles

1 Put a capo at the 1st fret to take the nut out of the equation.

2 Set the first string at a workable height – a 0.05in Allen wrench at the 21st fret is a good rough guide. This is the Allen key often provided for saddle adjustment.

4 Align the other saddles to the neck radius with an appropriate size radius gauge – in this case a modern 12in radius. If you don't have a radius gauge you could make one by tracing the fingerboard radius at the heel on to a piece of stiff card.

■ In the way of these things, having let the neck settle for a few days it's gone slightly concave, so a little truss rod adjustment may be required! See page 90 for this adjustment.

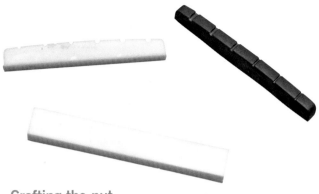

■ The plastic nut is slightly over-tight so will need to be gently sanded to size. I'm rubbing it on a fine wet and dry paper.

Crafting the nut

The simple nut is one of the most crucial elements in making a guitar work and sound well, and its success ensures the success of the whole guitar. There are a number of options here. We can either build a nut from a bone/horn blank, or adapt a preformed blank in bone, graphite or plastic. The latter is the easier option if you're just starting out. Regarding materials, bone and graphite are both self-lubricating, while Micarta is a sort of synthetic 'bone' but isn't self-lubricating.

■ This graphite impregnated nut is too tall and will need some material removing from the base. I find it easier to maintain a flat base on the nut by securing the file in a vice.

■ Adapting

Preformed nuts come in a range of widths, string spacings and materials. Some have a radiused bottom and others are flat, so check your guitar neck to see which you need.

The right height for the nut is partly about personal preference, but if the nut is too high you'll encounter intonation issues, particularly in the first position, while if it's too low you'll hear too much fret buzz. So file the base down to size slowly, constantly checking it in position with the strings in place.

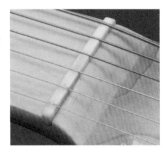

Both of these preformed nuts are workable if a little crude, as the string spacings aren't specific to this guitar or your style of playing.

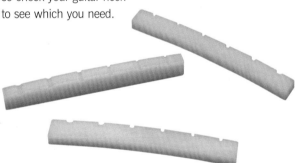

■ This particular nut slot has a flat bottom radius, so we need a flat-bottomed nut with a string spacing to suit the 43mm width. This JHS plastic nut is the right width and flat-bottomed, with pre-cut string spacings.

✎ Tech Tip

When a string binds in the nut slot, it makes a pinging sound as it breaks free of the slot. This ping is often attributed to the tremolo/vibrato, as it's the use of this device that triggers the release of the snagging. The nut will eventually need lubricating with graphite (a pencil tip will do).

John Diggins – Luthier

Shaping a nut from a blank

This is a harder but ultimately more satisfactory solution. I'm going to use a 'nut jig', a device that takes a lot of guesswork out of the process. The nut jig was designed by luthier Gary Carter and is a very versatile aid to making a nut for most types of guitar. If you do little of this kind of work then the jig provides a good template, while if you do a lot it's a great time saver.

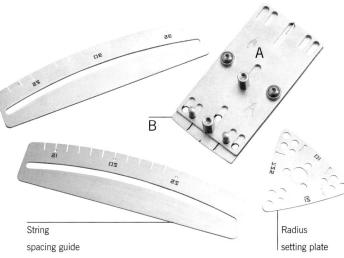

String
spacing guide

Radius
setting plate

1 Gauge the depth of the guitar's nut slot, ensuring plate B sits in the bottom of the nut slot, and lightly tighten the back nuts with the 8mm spanner/ wrench provided.

2 The differing heights of plates A and B now define the depth of the nut slot.

NB: If the nut slot has a flat bottom (as here), then plate A is used this way up. If it has a curved bottom you should reverse plate A. Also, don't be confused by the apparent upside-side down nature of the jig's radius at present, as we're just measuring the depth of the nut slot at the centre!

3 Check the guitar's fingerboard radius. The jig comes with a useful set of radius gauges. This guitar has a 12in radius.

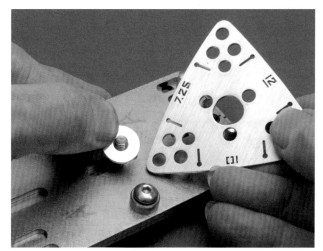

4 Install a washer and the appropriate radius setting plate, and loosely secure with the centre nut.

5 Clamp the assembled jig in a bench vice.

6 Mark the back of the nut blank at its centre and fit the nut in the slot at the top of the jig, aligning it with the centre line on the jig, securing the nut with the rear 'clamp' nut, and using any necessary washers. Ideally the setting plate will exhibit a slight flex at this point.

7 With a suitable file, roughly shape the nut leaving a minimum excess required for the nut string slots. Remove the nut and place in the neck slot.

8 Mark the position of the two outer strings on the nut – not too close to the edges of the fingerboard. A minimum 3mm allows for some first and sixth string vibrato. I prefer more, especially on the first string.

9 Fit a string spacing guide to the jig and align until you find a good match for your two outer strings. The spacing guide then automatically indicates the centres for the other strings.

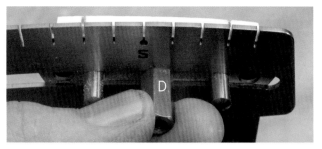

10 Tighten clamp D to fix the spacing guide.

11 Use the fine-toothed saw supplied to mark up the initial nut slots. and then remove the string spacing guide.

12 Using gauged nut files, file the slots to the height of the setting plate, with some relief at the back of the nut. File at a backward angle, as it's also necessary to shape the floor, or bottom, of the slot correctly, to enable the string to slide through it freely. If the slot isn't correctly shaped it'll prevent smooth tuning and will hamper the instrument's ability to return to tune, particularly after using the vibrato.

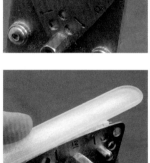

13 Finalise the shape of the nut with a finer toothed file – this is a cheap glass manicure file!

14 Trim the ends with an X-Acto fine blade saw. I tend to leave a tiny bit of excess at this stage, to allow some manoeuvre latitude when the strings are in place.

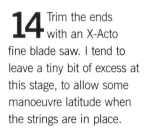

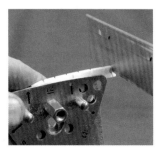

15 Final setting-up requires refitting the strings and then some fine tweaking for comfort, aesthetics and intonation.

16 If the nut still seems a little high the jig offers the facility to reduce this by measured amounts. Colour-coded wire gauges inserted beneath the nut raise it in increments of .0002in, from .008 to .020, and you then remove the excess from the top. Be aware that the thicker bass strings will require more excursion room than the treble strings. The wires are inserted in the jig as required.

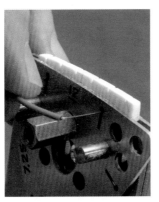

17 Once you're happy with the nut a small dab of Loctite is enough to hold it in place – this makes the nut easier to remove/replace later if necessary.

Without the aid of a nut jig

1 Beginning with an oversize bone blank, smooth the nut slot with a specialist 'nut seating file' specific to the slot size. It's important to avoid chipping the neck finish, so gently file the sharp edge of any lacquer and also file the nut bottom with 'in' strokes from both ends of the nut slot, thus avoiding accidentally pulling any lacquer from the neck.

2 Draw the fingerboard outline radius on the new nut with a sharp pencil.

3 Add a pencil radius above the fingerboard outline. This new radius needs to be enough to allow for the fret height, the string height and the thickness of the string (a guitar tech might add a little more for good measure). You'll certainly need to allow a little more height towards the bass strings, as they need slightly more room to vibrate without 'choking' on the 1st fret.

4 Using your pencil guidelines, carefully file the nut to its approximate required height.

5 If the nut is overly high a belt sander will make short work of bringing it down to size.

6 Measure your nut slot width and mark the required nut slots on your blank. Pay particular attention to the spacing of the sixth and first strings from the outside edge. Having strings too close to the edge will make finger vibrato difficult – 1/8in–1/16in from the edge may be enough depending on your playing style. Less first string vibrato requires less edge 'gap'!

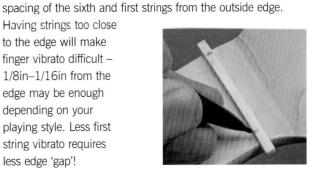

7 Kevin Ryan's string-spacing rule, available from Stewmac, is the easiest way to get even spacing between the outsides of adjacent strings – a more important factor than equal spacing at their centres. Use this rule to determine the position of the remaining string slots by lining up with your two outer slots and then marking up the four in the middle.

Surprisingly, expert luthiers often determine the individual string spacing by eye. This sounds a little unscientific, but the precise calculations in thousandths of an inch are made very complex by the fact that each string is a different gauge.

8 Check constantly for a snug and even fit in the nut slot. At this juncture the nut should still be left slightly overlong, for flexibility in the later stages of shaping. A 1/8in edge overlap will be enough to allow for some fine tuning.

9 You can position the first two 'outer' strings on the new nut by making pilot notches with a very fine craft saw (X-Acto or similar) with a blade of .010 gauge or less. You can then adopt the pro method to a degree by positioning the strings in very shallow pilot slots and then making any minor adjustments by eye before completing your actual filing of the final slots.

10 Then file the nut slots with gauged nut files appropriate to the gauge of strings you plan to use on the guitar.

11 Carefully trim and shape the nut with some regular files and the X-Acto saw.

12 Glue the new nut in place with a couple of dabs of superglue. Don't overdo the glue, as the nut may need to be removed again for correction. With the strings in place check the action at the 1st fret with the string depressed at the 3rd fret – a feeler gauge at the 1st fret should register approx .0035in. Adjust as required.

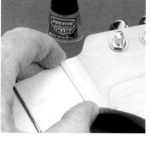

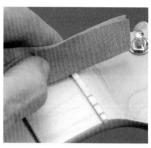

13 Polish the nut slots with some fine abrasive and lubricate with some graphite – a fine propelling pencil works well.

NB: If making a nut is proving difficult – and it can! – Stewmac offer a wide range of preformed bone nuts that are close to finished.

String tree

At this stage you may notice that the first string buzzes in the nut slot. This is because every 'S' type guitar exhibits a basic design fault – the straight neck/headstock alignment has no traditional break angle at the nut. This was solved by the original inventor by the addition of a washer and screw to pull down the first and second strings to the headstock, increasing the apparent break angle.

■ Since the late '50s this has evolved into a seagull-wing 'string tree' – sometimes simple, sometimes more sophisticated.

1 Site your string tree approximately halfway along the strings' headstock excursion and align so that a straight pull is maintained to the tuners. Make a start for the hole with a bradawl or a pilot drill – this is a modelmakers' drill.

2 Lubricate the back of the tree with a little Vaseline or ChapStick. This ensures no sticking during tuning and trem use – I'm using a Lubri-Kit syringe.

3 Attach the tree with a No '1' Phillips wood screw.

4 For the flame top maple guitar this modern streamlined tree may be more appropriate. This design also exerts less friction, which is good for keeping the guitar in tune. Please excuse the tatty strings – I initially set up guitars using these recycled strings, and then replace them with good strings. This saves ruining good strings in the process of removal and re-stringing!

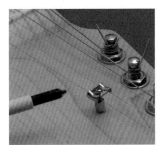

✒ Tech Tip

Never underestimate the strength of hard timber! Always pilot any screw holes in these tone woods with a drill gauged appropriately to the screw in use and always use the highest quality steel screws. The alternative can be broken screws becoming stuck in your guitar, which are difficult and time-consuming to extract.

John Diggins – Luthier

✒ Tech Tip

When drilling pilot holes in hard woods take your time and ease the drill in and out – otherwise the bit can easily snap in the timber, and is then difficult to extract.

John Diggins – Luthier

Strap buttons

This Stewmac body has been pre-drilled for standard late '50s strap positions. If there's any movement in the 1in No '6' Phillips raised countersunk screws, then a simple cocktail stick rawlplug will normally give more 'bite' to this vital fixing. A felt washer is a good way of protecting the brittle lacquer.

Trem cover

Site this carefully to ensure good access for stringing – there's a lot of leeway in the apparent position of this simple plate, but in fact a few millimetres can make a huge difference to convenient string access. Always position the plate with the strings at their intended pitch, as this will affect the trem block alignment considerably. The trem block will swing towards the neck if all the strings are de-tensioned – hence the oval holes for easier access in both eventualities.

Fix using ½in chrome No '4' raised countersunk screws, and do remember to pilot the holes with a 1.5mm drill.

Installation of the electrics

The pickups are perhaps the most significant factor contributing to the sound of your guitar. However, the other electrical elements – such as pots, switches and decent wiring – all play their part, so it's worth buying the best you can afford, both for initial tone and long-term reliability. In this section I'll look initially at the easiest pre-wired options, then at a very traditional 'S' type arrangement, a stacked humbucker approach, and the popular HSS humbucker and two single-coils. All the body, neck and pickup options discussed and shown are theoretically interchangeable, but I'll try to match ingredients for some acknowledged classic 'S' types you may want to use as a basis for your own guitar. A final option is the installation of a piezo-equipped bridge for 'acoustic' sounds.

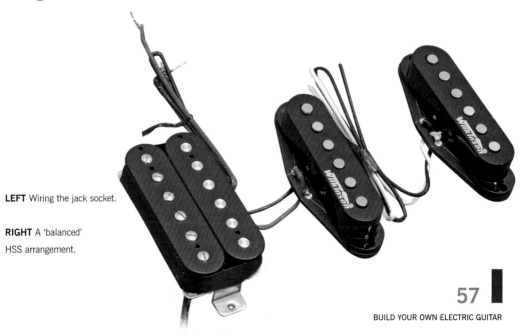

LEFT Wiring the jack socket.

RIGHT A 'balanced' HSS arrangement.

Pre-wired

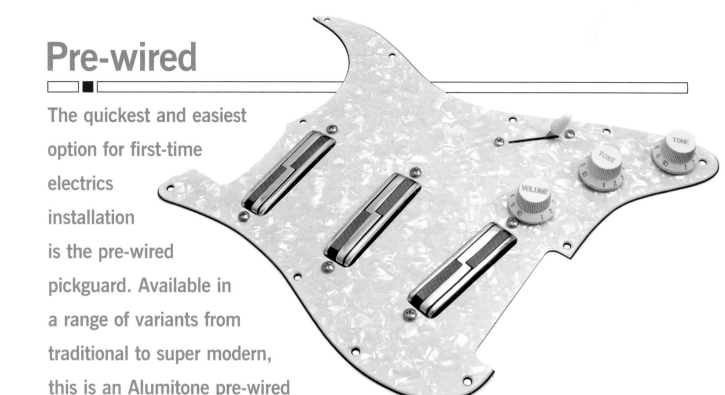

The quickest and easiest
option for first-time
electrics
installation
is the pre-wired
pickguard. Available in
a range of variants from
traditional to super modern,
this is an Alumitone pre-wired
from Don Lace. As well as quality 'low magnetic pull' pickups,
this rig also offers a high-quality switch and three high-grade pots.

1 Pre-tin your wires
with a little solder
to make the connections
easier. This just means
adding a little melted
solder to the bare wire
and letting it cool. Note
the useful third hand.

2 With a 25W soldering iron, connect your positive
output wire to the centre tag of the volume pot.
I'm using black for the positive wire – unconventional,
but OK if you're consistent!

3 Connect your negative
output (ground or screen)
to the the 'mid' tone pot.

4 Also connect a ground
wire attached to the
trem claw assembly to the
back of the tone pot.

5 Thread the output wires through to the jack socket cavity.

6 Allowing enough slack for easy access and maintenance, trim the wires to length.

7 Solder the tinned volume pot wire to the positive pole of your output jack...

8 ...and the ground to the outer pole of your jack socket.

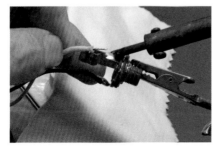

9 Attach the output jack to the jack plate with a socket spanner. This standard chrome plate is from Guitar Tech.

10 Pilot the fixing holes and screw into position with two No '4' ½in raised countersunk chromed screws.

11 We can now also attach the pickguard – piloting all the holes and fixing with No '4' ½in raised countersunk chrome screws. Take care not to foul the vibrato plate – you can jiggle the scratch plate position to give adequate clearance all round, and trim the guard if necessary with a small file.

Vintage-style

The 'vintage' style of
three single coils,
built from individual
components, offers
the most flexibility,
as you can choose each
pickup, pot and switch just as you
like them. If, for instance, you want to build
a guitar evoking an early '50s vibe the ingredients are all available.

Standard single coils: '50s era vintage

For the prized authentic '50s 'S' type sound we need staggered
Alnico magnet-single coils. These 'Golden Age' pickups from
Stewmac offer Alnico 5 magnets with designated pickups
for bridge, middle and neck, with corresponding
outputs and a nominal 6K resistance. They're
supplied with white and black plastic covers.

As a nod to modernism they're wired with
the middle PU (pickup) in opposite polarity
for a noise-cancelling benefit in positions two
and four of a now normal five-way switch.
Few players would want to return to a three-way
switch, but these pickups would function just as
well if you wanted that degree of authenticity.

Another sensible concession is the screening
foil around the coils, which should reduce some
unwanted noise induction.

1 Typically the early '50s 'S' type
featured a single-ply plastic
pickguard. This is a PG0550-125
from Allparts. It would sit well
with the ash body and maple neck
covered on page 18.

2 The single coils are screwed to the pickguard utilising the 6-32 UNC x ⅝in raised countersunk screws supplied and a No '1' Phillips driver. Typically the new guard may need a little countersinking to accommodate the screw head – but go easy, as these single-ply guards are brittle.

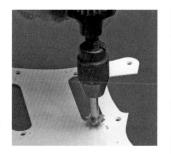

■ In traditional style the pickups are suspended with a silicone rubber spacer. Take care that the middle pickup (reverse polarity) is correctly sited.

3 Fit the five-way switch with another two 6-32 UNC ⅝in raised countersunk Phillips screws, 'spring side out'. Though a five-way switch wasn't typical until 1977 most early 'S' types have had one retro-fitted.

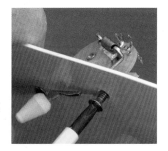

4 Fit the three 250K ohm pots – these are secured with a locking washer and a ½in socket spanner.

5 Tin the pickup wires and five-way switch inputs with a little solder and attach the pickup 'hot' wires as per the illustration above right and the picture below.

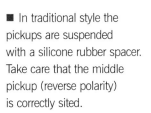

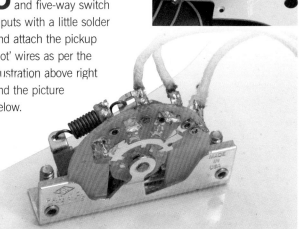

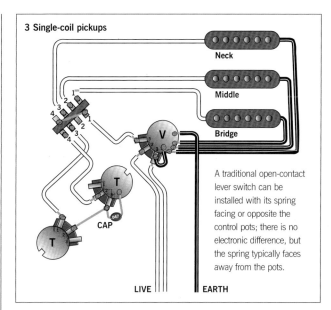

3 Single-coil pickups

Neck

Middle

Bridge

V

T

CAP

.047

T

A traditional open-contact lever switch can be installed with its spring facing or opposite the control pots; there is no electronic difference, but the spring typically faces away from the pots.

LIVE

EARTH

6 Solder the five-way bridge PU output pin one straight to the volume control.

7 Solder the pin three 'output' to the 'mid' tone control.

✏ Tech Tip

Using some RS Components' tinner cleaner on the tip of your soldering iron helps prevent the 'dry' joints that lead to poor earthing faults on many guitars.

John Diggins – Luthier

8 Solder the pin four output to the 'neck' tone control.

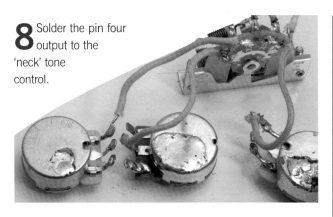

9 Bridge the pin four 'input' to the pin one output on the five-way switch.

10 Attach the PU ground or earth wires to the case of the volume control.

11 'Loop' the volume control ground to the neck and mid tone controls. This is 'belt-and-braces', but advisable – especially when there is no screening plate on the pickguard.

12 Introduce a .05mfd capacitor from solder tag three of the neck tone control to ground on the back of the pot and the mid tag of the 'mid' tone control.

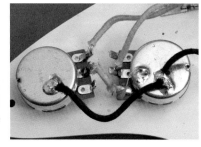

13 Ground the third tag of the volume control to the back of the pot...

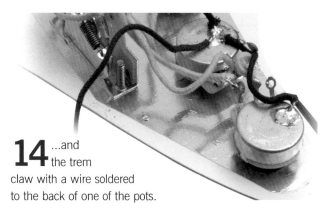

14 ...and the trem claw with a wire soldered to the back of one of the pots.

15 Connect a positive output wire from the mid tag of the volume control, thread this through to the output cavity, and connect a ground output wire from the 'mid' tone control case or volume case.

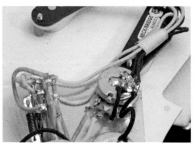

16 Also thread through to the output cavity.

17 Tidy the cable looms and tape up before installing the pickguard.

Tech Tip

Set the initial pickup heights with consideration for the greater excursion of the strings at the neck position, tending to more output – fine tuning of the heights will then depend on your playing style. Never set pickups so close to the strings that the magnetic field interferes with their natural excursion. This will result in wolf notes, 'beats' and odd harmonics.

John Diggins – Luthier

18 Solder the positive wire to the tip of the output jack and the ground to the sleeve connection. The output jack is attached to the recessed jack plate with a locking washer and ½in nut.

19 Screw the jack plate to the guitar body with two piloted No '4' ½in raised countersunk screws.

Tech Tip

In standard wiring, the pole '0' is always live and the '1', '3' and '5' connections are made or broken by the switch.

John Diggins – Luthier

20 Pilot the holes and attach the pickguard using No '4' ½in raised countersunk screws.

■ Below is a useful guide to five-way switching arrangements.

Understanding the 5-position selector switch

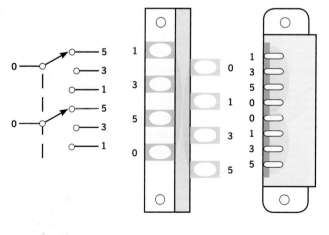

Schematic　　　　Vintage-type　　　　Inline-type

Modern 'stacked' humbuckers & lace sensors

Since the first 'S' types were designed, our world has become a lot noisier in the RF spectrum. Radio microphones, dimmers and mobile phones all compete for attention and find their way into our guitar. Recent designs can help.

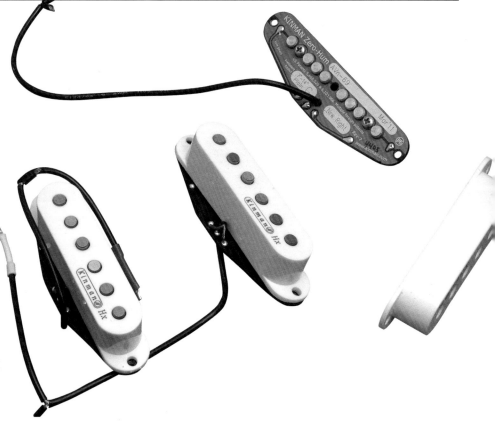

Kinman

The Australian company Kinman offer a fascinating range of modern low-noise but authentically shaped single coils. These wire up exactly like standard vintage single coils but with the advantage of a humbucker circuit. The two coils are 'stacked' instead of sitting physically parallel as in a familiar PAF humbucker.

For traditional five-way wiring you could use the wiring scheme on page 61. However, I'm going to wire these Kinmans as 'the magnificent seven'. This gives us seven-way switching in an 'invisible' arrangement that still utilises a familiar five-way switch. The only addition is a push-pull pot. This works exactly like a normal volume or tone control but also incorporates a switch. This sits in one of the vintage pot 'slots' but offers the additional versatility of:

Sound 6 – the 'David Gilmour' sound; neck and bridge pickups together.
Sound 7 – all three pickups together – similar to a Brian May approach (though his three pickups are normally wired in series).

Be aware that some 'S' type bodies may need a small additional cavity routing to accommodate the 1.25in depth of the push-pull pot.

1 Fit the three pickups to a standard modern three-ply pickguard – I'm using a Stewmac mint-tinted guard for a '60s look, which will sit well with this guitar's Sonic Blue body and a Warmoth 'licensed' rosewood board '60s era neck.

Ideally I'd exchange the new white Kinman plastic PU cases with these tinted vintage types – it's important when doing this to remove the cases very carefully to avoid damage to the Kinmans' shielding. Note, however, that these stacked humbuckers are deeper than regular single coils and have slightly different pole spacings, so we'll need specific Kinman vintage covers.

The pickups are seated traditionally, using silicone 'rubber' isolation suspensions and No '1' Phillips 6-32 machine screws.

Take care to get these noiseless pickups in the right pickup slots. The pickup engraved with 'Nrw' (narrow) is for the neck position (long cable), 'Int' is intermediate for the middle position (mid-length cable), and 'Std' is standard for the bridge position (short cable).

2 Adjust the mounting screws so the PU is held firmly by the silicone tubes. The screws are deliberately tight and will squeak.

3 Fit the pots, including the push-pull in place of the lower tone control (this is the easiest position for practical playing access if you have a trem arm on your guitar).

4 All the pots on a single-coil guitar should have a nominal 250K ohm value. The split-shaft type are often preferred.

5 The pots simply slot through the pickguard with a locking washer to keep the pot from revolving, and then you tighten the external nut, which usually requires a ½in socket wrench.

The push-pull pot in position. It helps if you think of this as a normal pot with a switch as a piggy-back addition.

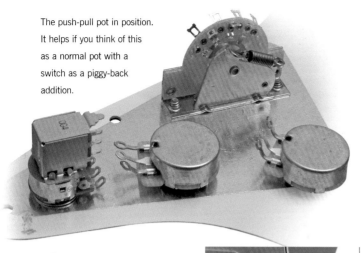

6 Position the five-way switch this way up, spring side close to the pickups, and lock in place with the two 6-32 UNC ⅝in raised countersunk screws supplied.

7 Tin all the connectors and wire up the pickups to the five-way switch at lugs 123 as shown in the diagram on page 61 and the picture here. Note that the five-way switch is reversed for this guitar.

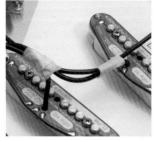

8 Wire the ground from the three pickups to the rear case of the volume pot. Taping up the wiring loom will make it easier to position the pickguard on the guitar.

9 Wire up the bridge pickup to the push-pull switch. Pins one and two give 'normal' wiring when the pot is 'up'.

10 Wire the five-way switch to the volume pot and the 'mid' tone control as usual (see page 62).

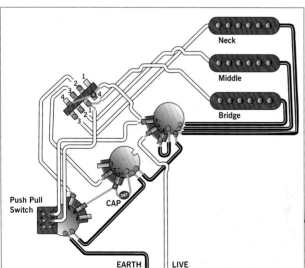

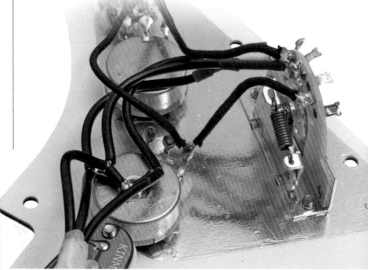

11 Wire the 'loop' across the two sides of the five-way. This is definitely 'guitar-player' soldering!

12 Wire a .047 capacitor to ground on the back of the 'neck' tone control – the tweezers act as a heat sink – and wire the 'mid' pickup tone control to the capacitor.

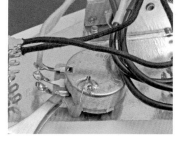

13 Link the two tone controls.

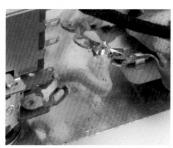

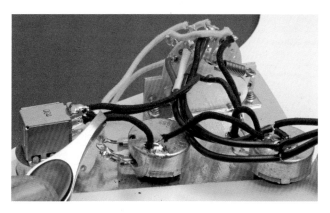

14 Wire the common 'ground' or earth wires to the back plates of the controls. Kinman prefer to wire a shielded cable to the back of the volume control and solder the hot output (mid tag) of the volume control.

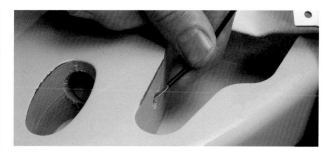

15 Thread the screened cable though to the output jack recess. These can then be connected, 'red' to the hot (tip) connection of the output jack and 'ground' to the sleeve connection.

16 Last but not least it's important to ground the cable attached to the trem claw that earths the strings. I'm utilising the case of the tone control as a ground.

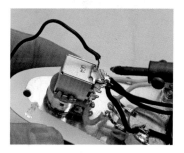

Lace sensor golds

Another modern pickup option worth considering is 'lace sensors', as used for much of Eric Clapton's classic work. Currently these wire exactly the same as vintage pickups except that they have an extra shielding ground for each pickup – this simply means wiring up the orange cables to 'hot' while the green and white cables both go to ground.

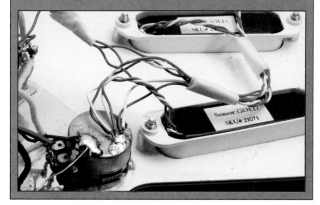

Humbucker and single-coil arrangements

A popular modern arrangement combines the single coil character of the 'S' type with the versatility of a conventional humbucker in the bridge position. This can either be used normally or 'split coil', giving the option of returning to a standard three single coils at the flick of a switch.

If you decide to go along this pickup route then choose a body ready-routed for humbuckers or professionally routed by a local luthier – I'd strongly suggest you avoid trying to bodge a rout with a hammer and chisel – body splits and cracks in the finish are easy to effect and expensive to repair.

Audio balance

As a humbucker tends to give a higher output than vintage single coils, one critical issue to consider is audio balance. Wilkinson is one manufacturer that offers single coils specifically designed to balance in an HSS arrangement.

Other options to consider include 'a four-wire' output humbucker, which offers the extra versatility of wiring the humbucker coils in 'series' – parallel, in phase or out of phase etc. These options can be made switchable by adding push-pull pots or a superswitch to the circuit.

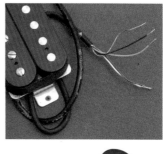

■ You may prefer a black pickguard and pickup covers, depending on your guitar colour. All these parts are available in a range of finishes.

A standard HSS arrangement

1 Fit the single-coil pickups as normal, taking care to install them as designated ('middle' and 'neck'), as these often

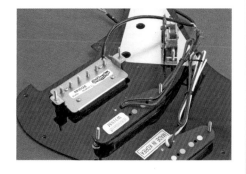

have different outputs and may be different polarities. The humbucker needs to be fitted the correct way round, with the cables orientated to the control cut-out. Figure 3 shows a recommended HSS wiring arrangement with 'coil cut' in position four, giving bridge and middle as two single coils in parallel.

2 Wire the rest of the pickups as per the illustration below. The only critical factor in fitting the pickups was the length

of the height adjustment screws. These all had to be reduced by ¼in to fit within the cavity – I did this with a junior metalworkers' hacksaw.

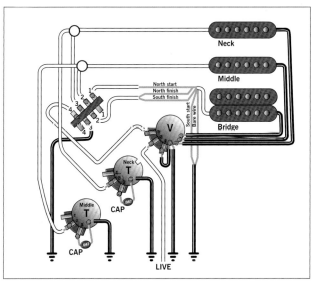

Alternate wirings

For alternate wirings you could install a push-pull pot as shown on page 64. The Stewmac diagram below shows the potential configurations obtainable from a four-wire humbucker.

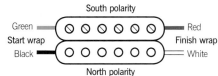

Colour	Coil	Standard	Parallel
Black	North start	Hot	Hot
White	North finish	Solder w/red	Ground w/bare
Green	South start	Ground w/bare	Ground w/bare
Red	South finish	Solder w/white	Hot
Bare	Ground	Bare w/green	Ground w/bare

Another alternative is to install a four-pole superswitch, which under the guise of a conventional five-way switch can provide numerous options, limited only by your imagination. Circuitry varies, so follow the diagram supplied with your specific superswitch. The same applies to pickup wiring, which varies from manufacturer to manufacturer, all of whom adopt different colour codes.

Be adventurous, though I'd strongly suggest that you keep a stage guitar as simple as possible and reserve the more complex switching for studio use – you have enough to think about on stage already!

Installing piezo saddles

If you need a very versatile electric guitar a currently popular option is to add an 'acoustic' guitar output by installing piezo sensors in the bridge. This is now relatively easy to achieve, with kits available from several companies including the Graph Tech 'Ghost' unit.

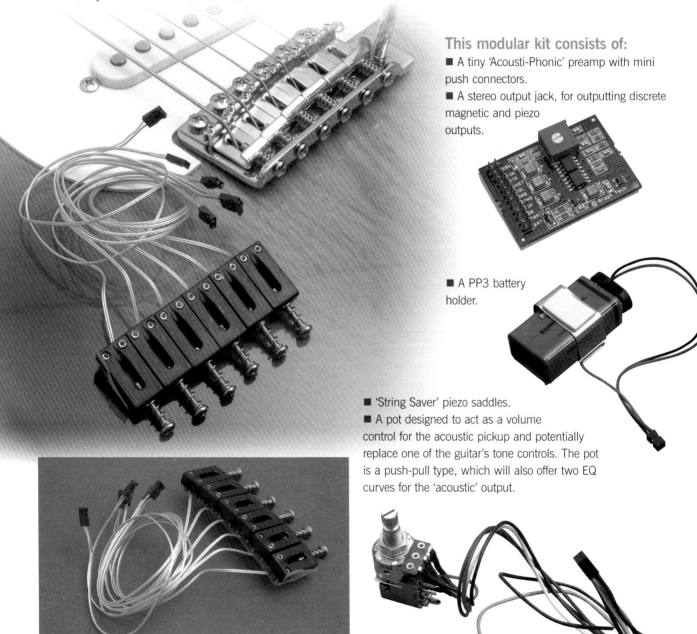

This modular kit consists of:
■ A tiny 'Acousti-Phonic' preamp with mini push connectors.
■ A stereo output jack, for outputting discrete magnetic and piezo outputs.

■ A PP3 battery holder.

■ 'String Saver' piezo saddles.
■ A pot designed to act as a volume control for the acoustic pickup and potentially replace one of the guitar's tone controls. The pot is a push-pull type, which will also offer two EQ curves for the 'acoustic' output.

Planning

Here I'm going to fit the piezo to this 'humbucker cut-out' body, which can easily accommodate the preamp. This will result in one guitar producing single-coil, humbucker and acoustic outputs – very versatile!

The kit is so small that it may fit inside your new guitar with little adjustment. Though the PP3 could also conceivably go in this space it would mean removing the strings and pickguard to change the battery, therefore I'll install the battery in the trem compartment, following the example of Pete Townshend and Eric Clapton.

You can choose if you want to wire the guitar with a separate 'acoustic' output or a blend pot. You can also install a MIDI output (if you purchase another board).

For this installation I'm going for the separate acoustic output only, which I'll route to an 'acoustic' amp. I'll also install the push-pull pot for EQ and volume on the acoustic output.

Installation

1 If you've already installed and set up a conventional bridge make a note of the current saddle heights and string lengths, as this will save time on assembly.

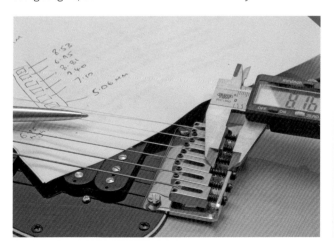

2 Remove and replace the saddles.

3 Check the available space in your guitar body for the associated electronics.

4 Fit the stereo jack in place of the mono one.

5 Mark up the pickguard at the point where the output wires will need to enter the pickup cavity. A chinagraph pencil works best on the shiny plastic. To get accurate markings do this with the trem and pickguard in place.

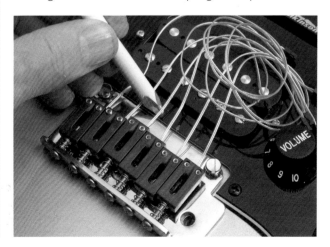

6 Notch the pickguard to accommodate the thickness of the piezo output wires – I'm using a needle file and protecting the installed pickups with a plastic 'mask' secured with masking tape.

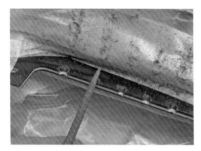

7 I'm also making small channels in the body with a craft saw and needle files to avoid any danger of pinching these frail connectors when the pickguard is replaced.

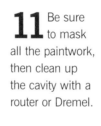

8 Protect the guitar body front with some bubblewrap...

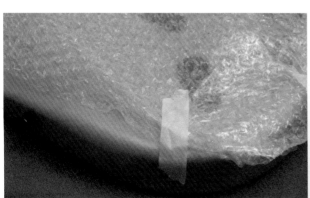

9 ...and mark up the rear cavity that's required, using a PP3 battery as a template.

10 Drill out the major part of the space required, taking care not to drill through to the other side!

11 Be sure to mask all the paintwork, then clean up the cavity with a router or Dremel.

12 Finish up with some abrasive...

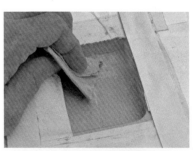

13 ...and perhaps paint the cavity to make it look tidier.

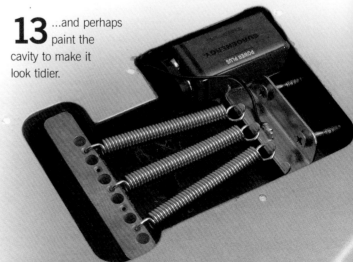

14 I'm replacing the 'mid' tone control with the acoustic volume pot. This push-pull volume/tone pot requires 5mm more depth to the control cavity – I marked the position of the cavity by removing the existing pot and pushing a bradawl through the existing pickguard hole.

15 I'm minimising the cavity by drilling a 24mm localised hole rather than more extensive routing. As I don't possess a router capable of working in this enclosed cavity I hand-chiselled the drilled hole and then finished off with a drum sander.

16 I'm going to fix the preamp to the back of the pickguard, which is OK with Graph Tech. However, I'll make the tricky connections before sticking it down.

17 The saddle connections are all simple push-fits into a parallel strip; and then another push-fit cable, which is clearly labelled, links to the main board.

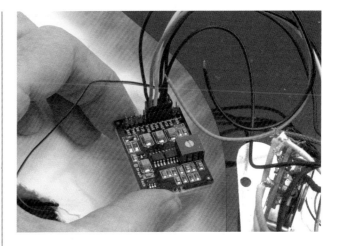

18 The supplied push-pull pot is connected to the main board with a four-way push-fit connector.

19 The green wire from the push-pull pot loom is now wired to the centre pin of the volume pot for your magnetic pickups.

20 The supplied output loom is threaded through to the jack recess and soldered to the stereo output jack, using a set of colour-coded wires.

21 The ouput loom's push-fit connector is attached to the main board.

22 An extra (black) ground wire from this loom is designed for the strings via the usual trem claw solder connection.

73

23 The battery wires are fed through to the pickup cavity.

24 These also push-fit to the main board. To ensure the polarity, put the black wire on the ground side of the connectors.

Does it work?

Yes, it works just as well as the Pete Townshend Strat I had when I wrote the *Fender Stratocaster Manual*, so it's a useful tool if you need an acoustic simulation in a hurry! I also prefer having the volume control on the pickguard rather than as an addition.

I intend to use a splitter box for the stereo jack output and wire two mono outputs from that for a standard electric amp and an acoustic amp or PA feed – again as Pete Townshend.

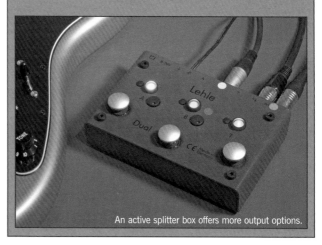

An active splitter box offers more output options.

25 I'll now fix the board in place by means of its self-adhesive base. Although the control space is very crowded it's just workable!

26 Replace the pickguard.

LEFT A splitter box with an OEP audio-isolating transformer will avoid earth loops when using two amps.

New trem cover

I did, however, have to make a custom-size trem cover for the space left by the slightly larger trem/PP3 cavity, as follows:

1 I marked up the size based on the old cover, adding a couple of millimetres to the width. The new cover is cut from single-ply black pickguard plastic from WD Music.

2 I cut this roughly to size with a fretsaw...

3 ...and smoothed the edges, initially with a Surform tool and then some Microplane shapers, with a straight edge as a reference.

4 The string access hole I drilled out and then shaped with a fret saw...

5 ...some sanding sticks and a rat tail file.

6 I finished it with some 3M fine grade polishing paper wrapped on a stick, which also worked well for polishing the edges.

7 The screw holes were templated from the old (slightly too small) trem cover with a bradawl...

8 ...and then drilled and countersunk.

9 The finished plate looks fine!

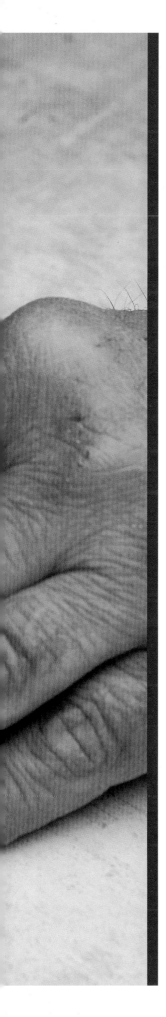

Assembly and fitting 2: unfinished components

If you have access to the required spray shop you may want to build your guitar from raw, unfinished timber components. It's relatively easy to obtain ash, alder and exotic hardwood bodies and maple necks. Beware, however, of the dangers inherent in inhalation of abrasive debris and cellulose and urethane finishes.

If in doubt consult a local body shop and supervise a custom finish the safe way. Some spray shops will let you do some of the work yourself, subject to supervision and appropriate health and safety precautions.

Even if you decide to hand the fine work and safety hazards to a professional there's much you can do by way of preparation and finishing in your home workshop.

LEFT Routing a headstock.

RIGHT Tuners and bushings.

Wood preparation and finish

The lovely grain patterns in raw ash are notoriously difficult to work – it's one of the reasons many makers switched to alder for their guitar bodies. The open grain must be filled before lacquering.

1 Sand the guitar body with 3M180-grit Free-Cut abrasive paper. The aim is to make the surface as smooth as possible before applying the filler. Always sand in the direction of the grain, to avoid unnecessarily 'raising' it.

2 Once the surface feels smooth to the touch, sand the guitar one more time with 240-grit Free-Cut abrasive. Free-Cut is a favourite with luthiers due to its non-clogging characteristics.

3 Wipe the guitar with a soft lint-free cloth to remove the sanding dust. Go over the guitar again to remove fingerprints and any oily residues.

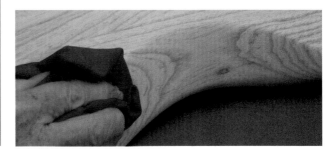

4 To seal and prepare the surface of the guitar for the lacquer topcoat, luthier John Diggins recommends a dilute blend of white and maple Brummer interior wood filler.

5 Mix the filler, adding a little water for flexibility. Apply with a lint-free rag, rubbing into any raised grain or minute cracks.

6 Sand the guitar with 240 Free-Cut after the sealer has completely dried and then repeat the process.

7 Mark up a centred hole, which will eventually be utilised for the strap button.

8 Start the hole with a bradawl and then pre-drill.

9 In the workshop I used a large wood screw in the strap hole and a custom-made neck bracket to suspend the guitar body in a revolving 'spit' – the neck bracket is held with two drywall phosphated screws, which are stronger than conventional wood screws. Suspending the guitar makes it easy to apply the lacquer and the slow revolutions avoid gravity causing drip patterns in the lacquer.

10 John, totally kitted out to avoid lacquer inhalation, first applied four thin coats of sanding sealer – Becker Acroma NL2004 pre-catalysed lacquer.

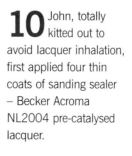

11 He then applied six coats of NM2502-0090 Syntema clear nitrocellulose lacquer. Applying a light coat prevents drips, runs and heavy spots from building up on the guitar. Allow each coat to completely dry – which only means waiting about 20 minutes at normal room temperature.

12 John custom-mixed the colours for the '50s-style two-colour sunburst, using the Syntema clear nitrocellulose as a base and adding Axminster-supplied tints 'to taste' for the black and yellow layers.

13 John first applied the black-stained lacquer to the edges, allowed this to dry and then flatted it down with some light 400-grit freecut paper.

14 He then applied the 'yellow'.

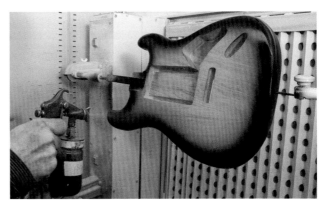

15 Finally the 'burst' is applied as a separate layer and sealed wth three coats of clear lacquer. The guitar finish is best left to harden for a week – still suspended to avoid any contact damage.

16 Once hardened the finish is lightly sanded with 1200-grit 'wet and dry', lightly lubricated with white spirit, as this removes any slight pocks in the lacquer surface.

17 The guitar finish is then polished with T-Cut on a rag, using a circular motion. Allow the T-Cut to dry to a white mist then polish off.

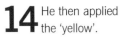

Neck finishing

The maple neck of the guitar doesn't require wood filler sealing so we can progress directly to lacquering. A rosewood fingerboard requires some careful masking, as we don't want nitro on the playing surface. However, a maple neck and fingerboard can be fully finished without masking. I'm preparing several necks here for optional assemblies.

1 The necks are mounted in a custom-made revolving jig within the same dust-free and extractor-fan equipped spraying tent. John has adapted his jig to take a standard truss-rod thread. Revolving facilitates even spraying and the extractors protect John's lungs and control dust.

2 The nitrocellulose base coat is applied using a fine spray on the revolving neck. This is allowed to dry for several hours. A rub down with 400-grit abrasive achieves a key for the second base coat. This is applied and allowed to dry.

3 The final coat of a darker 'pre-aged' nitrocellulose is applied using a specially designed (pre-CBS) mustard jar spray container. Two coats of clear lacquer seal the surface.

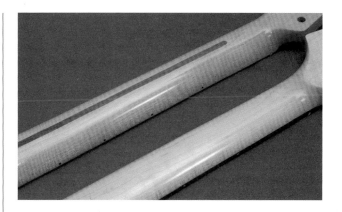

4 The almost dry necks now look fantastic if a little 'over shiny', and are put in a special drying cupboard overnight.

5 Once the lacquer has hardened the necks are lightly sanded with 1200 wet and dry lubricated with some white spirit...

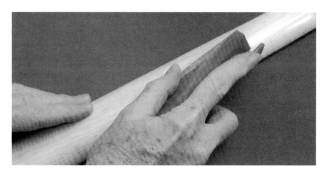

6 ...and then gently buffed with T-Cut automobile restorer. Apply a thin coat of the T-Cut with a rag, allow to dry and then polish off with a clean cotton rag as with the body.

Vintage-style 'S' types assembly

'50s- and '60s-style 'S' types are assembled and aligned following the same guidelines as the 'easy assemble' guitar on pages 40 – with, however, some slight differences:

Tuners

The headstocks for licensed Warmoth '50s and '60s 'S' type necks are designed for lightweight Kluson machines. These require a simple push-fit bushing arrangement.

1 Often the holes are slightly undersize and require a little careful enlarging with a peg router – we're looking for a snug fit, so don't overdo the enlarging! A gentle tap with a rubber hammer secures the ferrule.

2 The machines are then positioned, pilot-holed for the screws and fixed with No '3' ⅜in round-head nickel-plated steel Phillips screws.

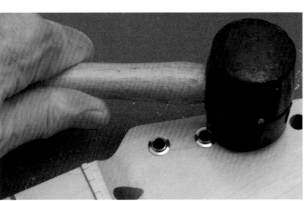

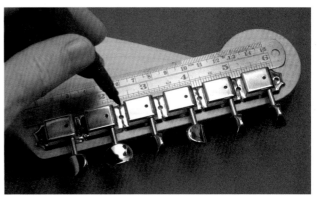

■ These cunning tuning machines from Stewmac look the 'vintage slot-head' business, but are actually an automatic locking design for better tuning stability – brilliant!

■ Another option to consider is these Kluson-alikes from Guitar Tech, which offer two post holes for variable break angles.

String trees

■ A '50s-style guitar often has an unusual type of string tree improvised from a stray washer fitted with a No '3' Phillips ⅜in round-head.

■ A '60s-style guitar has a seagull-wing string tree fitted with a similar screw.

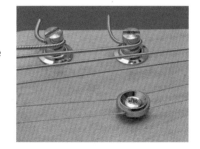

Strap buttons

The rear button fits easily into the hole utilised for the spray-booth bracket. The top horn button I'm fitting in the early '50s position – the No '6' screw needs to be piloted with a ³⁄₃₂in drill.

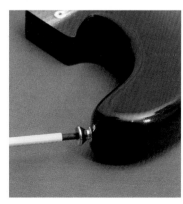

Pilot holes

Never underestimate the need for pilot holes in these hard woods. The rule of thumb for screw pilot hole depths in hard woods is 'equal to the length of the screw thread'.

Drilling/sizing considerations for wood screws

The following chart will help you drill the proper-sized holes to achieve maximum holding power in hard woods:

Screw size	Pilot hole in hard woods
3	¹⁄₁₆ in
4	⁵⁄₆₄ in
5	³⁄₃₂ in
6	³⁄₃₂ in
7	⁷⁄₆₄ in
8	⁷⁄₆₄ in

Not drilling a pilot hole will result in broken screws, split timber and much time wasted in extracting broken screws.

Trem set

Normally three springs would suffice in the floating trem arrangement with modern 009-042 light gauge strings; however, for this '50s-style guitar I'm fitting period correct 012-056 heavy gauge strings and using the original concept of five retaining springs.

Neck bolts

1 Many bodies that are supplied unfinished aren't pre-drilled for neck bolts. A good tip for aligning with a pre-drilled neck is to position some short round-head screws in the neck holes.

2 A little wax crayon is rubbed on to the screws.

3 Line the neck socket with some masking tape. Then press the neck in place in the neck socket, leaving a guide impression for the correct siting of the body holes.

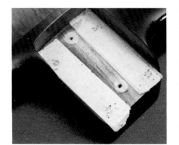

4 Firm these up with a bradawl and test your sitings for correct alignment by inserting matchsticks in the bradawl holes – they should line up perfectly with the pre-drilled neck holes.

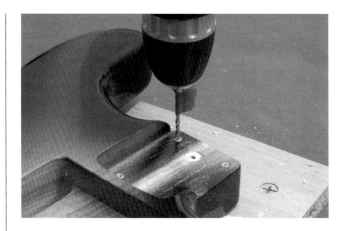

5 You can then carefully drill through the body in the neck pocket using first a ⅛in drill. I'm not going totally through to the external finish, just far enough to make an impression – the red tape acts as a depth guide.

6 Complete the holes from the finish side with a sharp bradawl. This avoids cracking and flaking of the lacquer.

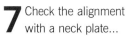

7 Check the alignment with a neck plate...

8 ...and if correct enlarge the holes with a ³⁄₁₆in drill, protecting the lacquer with some masking tape.

9 Attach the neck as on page 44. Don't forget to candle-wax the screws!

Headstock shaping

The maple-top guitar from Assembly and Fitting 1 has been fitted with a Stewmac maple neck purposely supplied with an oversize and unshaped headstock for custom finishing.

Be aware that the familiar 'S' type headstock shape may be subject to trademarks and copyright, though licensed versions are available. John Diggins shaped this headstock to a Stauffer/Bigsby-like shape, but with a custom adjustment:

1 He first adhered the roughly shaped headstock to a standard template with double-sided tape. Next he drew a rough outline.

2 John used a pin router to achieve an even cut-out, and has padded out the guide pin to give a bit more leeway in the final shaping.

3 The routing is done in gradual steps to avoid damage.

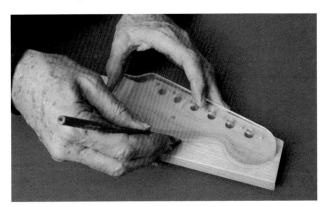

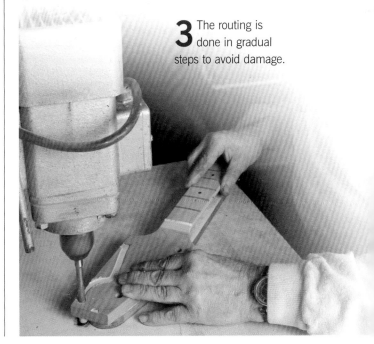

4 Any excess timber is removed with a band saw.

5 John made up a custom shaping rasp using some self-adhesive 80-grit Free-Cut paper on a piece of scrap wood, moving down to 180-grit for finishing.

6 I drew a custom 'bite' shape on some masking tape for an approximate outline.

7 John made a router guide based on this.

8 This was attached to the underside of the headstock, and John then routed the headstock from above.

9 I cleaned up the surface with some Free-Cut paper, purposely leaving the 'bite' a little ragged.

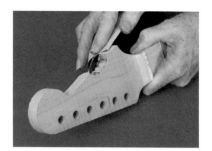

10 The raw timber surfaces are touched up with a little clear nitrocellulose applied from a rag.

■ I like the offbeat effect of the new unconventional headstock – a 'tasty' neck.

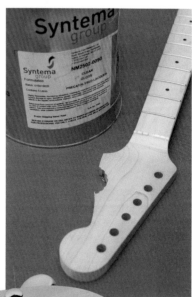

A fret polish – different approaches

As with most new frets the Stewmac neck for the maple-cap guitar requires a little polish. The fretting itself is very accurate when checked with a straight edge – there are no proud frets or noticeable 'dips'.

The time-honoured way to polish your frets is with diminishing grades of wire wool and fine abrasive paper coupled with a fingerboard guard.

■ Wearing protective gloves and eye protection, carefully dress the frets with some 000 grade wire wool. Beware of overdoing this, as you can change the shape of the frets and cause much worse problems. Remove the masking tape.

■ A light finishing polish with a lambswool buffer is good for a maple fingerboard, while the finish on a rosewood fingerboard will respond to a light application of a little lemon oil. This will also help remove any adhesive deposit left by the tape.

An alternative approach

A more modern method that saves engaging with the potential dangers of wire wool fragments is to use 'fret erasers' – rubber blocks colour-coded with fine abrasive. These come in five grits, 180–1000. I'm starting with the 180 and working down to the 1000 for a fine polish. It's important to mask the maple fingerboard with masking tape or a fret guard.

■ Here I'm using a self-adhesive Scary Creative template, which is a great time-saver.

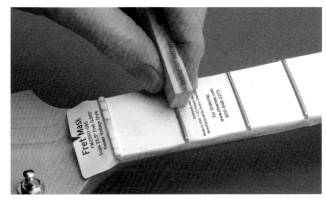

BUILD YOUR OWN ELECTRIC GUITAR

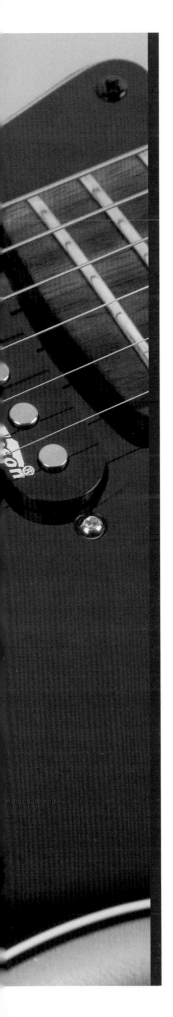

Set-up is everything!

We could have the world's greatest ingredients – the finest woods and the most superb electrics – and still end up with a poor, unplayable guitar. The most important aspect of any guitar is not price but set-up.

Perhaps surprisingly the most important working components on the guitar are the strings. These need to be chosen carefully and set up so that the guitar plays in tune, thereby ensuring that playing it is a pleasure.

Pickups need to be aligned for balance across the strings and between pickup combinations. Everything that moves needs to be lubricated.

LEFT A balanced set of single coil and humbuckers.

RIGHT A modern Wilkinson trem and steel block.

89

Neck alignment and truss rod adjustment

Neck alignment is a critical factor in the initial set-up of any new guitar.
With a bolt-on neck there's scope for adjustment by altering the pitch
of the neck in relation to the body.

Why would you want to do this?

The need to adjust the pitch of the neck usually occurs in situations where the string height is high and the saddle adjustment is as low as possible.

In practice a wooden 'shim' approximately .010in (0.25mm) thick is often placed in the neck pocket, underneath the end of the neck.

A new shim approximately ½in (12.8mm) wide x 1¾in (44.5mm) long x .010in (0.25mm) thick will allow you to raise the action at the saddles approximately ¹⁄₃₂in (0.8mm).

Tech Tip

If you can't achieve a workable action with the grub screws set at their lowest then you probably need a shim in the neck cavity. Also, a good rough guide for action setting is to put a .50in Allen key under the 21st fret – if it fits, the action's in the right area.

John Diggins – Luthier

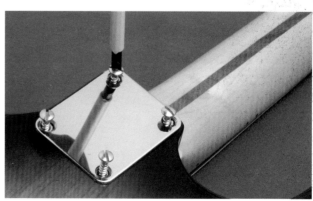

1 Slacken the strings and unscrew the four neck screws using a No '2' Phillips screwdriver or a 7mm straight-slot. Ease the neck gently from its seating in the pocket of the body.

2 Make a shim ½in (12.8mm) wide x 1¾in (44.5mm) long x .010in (0.25mm) thick from a scrap of wood veneer.

3 Place the shim in position towards the rear of the pocket, with a tiny dab of glue to hold it in place, and carefully replace the neck and retighten the neck fixing screws.

Truss rod initial set-up

New necks are often supplied with very little tension in the truss rod and you can't really tell if it needs adjustment until the guitar is strung at tension for a few days. The 'Standard' vintage-type truss rod can counteract concave curvature, or a neck that has too much relief, by generating a force in the neck opposite to that caused by excessive string tension.

1 Slacken the strings. Then, using a No '2' Phillips screwdriver, carefully unscrew the four neck bolts approximately ⅛in at the top and 1in at the 'back' – this should be enough to tilt the neck back for access to the truss rod screw.

A Warmoth neck

Unusually this neck and body arrangement resulted in too much back angle and an impossibly low action.

The solution is a reverse shim at the front of the neck socket, pitching the neck 'up' from the body. This does the trick, though there's now quite a lot of fine work needed on the saddles to fine tune the radius and intonation.

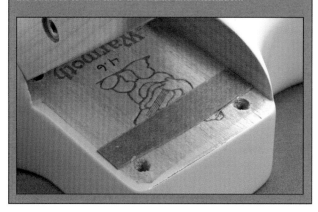

NB: If present be very careful to note the position of any neck shims (small slivers of wood or card in the neck pocket), as they must remain in the same position when the neck is reseated.

Access to the truss rod on vintage '50s and '60s 'S' types varies, as some have a small cut-out indentation in the pickguard to enable easier access. Generally the earliest guitars and their reissues don't have this. With these guitars you may have to unscrew the neck bolts slightly more to access the truss rod and avoid the risk of damaging the pickguard.

2 Adjust the truss rod screw a quarter-turn clockwise.

NB: Although this is really a job for a straight-slot 8mm or $^{11}/_{32}$in screwdriver, with the difficult access involved a No '2' Phillips often works well and risks less damage to the plastic pickguard.

Alternatively, if the neck is too convex (strings too close to the fingerboard), turn the truss rod nut a quarter-turn anticlockwise to allow the string tension to pull more relief into the neck.

NB: For obvious reasons the vintage truss rod was originally conceived to adjust situations with too much relief – it is much more likely to be successful in this application. A modern bi-flex rod will put pressure on the neck in either situation.

3 Checking that any shims are correctly reseated, replace the neck and re-tension the strings to correct pitch.

Adjustment at the headstock

Many modern necks have easier access to the truss rod at the headstock. Note that the required Allen key size varies depending on the neck model and date.

First look along the edge of the fingerboard from behind the headstock toward the body of the instrument. A slight concave in the neck with the strings at tension is normal and essential to enable the strings' normal excursion.

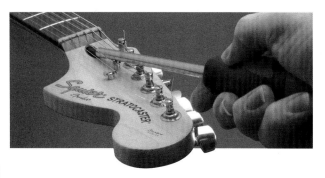

Modern Warmoth necks

The modern Warmoth neck has a very individual 'Gotoh' approach, with two points of adjustment for the truss rod. This requires a different approach:

1 Tighten the rod at the heel conventionally before fitting the neck and applying string tension. This requires a 5.5mm Allen key – tighten until the neck tests flat with a straight edge.

2 Fit the neck and string the guitar.

3 If the rod still needs adjustment this can be done at the side with a 3mm Allen, though Warmoth insist that the adjustment be done with the strings de-tensioned.

If the neck seems too concave or convex, turn the truss rod nut clockwise to remove excess relief. If the neck is too convex (strings too close to the fingerboard), turn the truss rod nut anticlockwise to allow the string tension to pull more relief into the neck. Check your tuning, then recheck the relief and readjust as needed.

NB: In either case, if you meet excessive resistance when adjusting the truss rod, or your instrument seems to need constant adjustment, or adjusting the truss rod has no effect on the neck, take the instrument to a qualified guitar tech.

Recommended neck relief	
Neck radius	Relief
7.25in	.012in (0.3mm)
9.5 to 12in	.010in (0.25mm)
15 to 17in	.008in (0.2mm)

Fine set-up of the nut

The set-up of the nut is a crucial element of a good guitar. When it's wrong the guitar can rattle and buzz and won't play in tune – strings stick and the trem may appear to cause tuning problems. Beyond not being 'too' high – which often causes intonation problems – a lot of what constitutes the 'correct' height for nut slots is all about individual preference and feel.

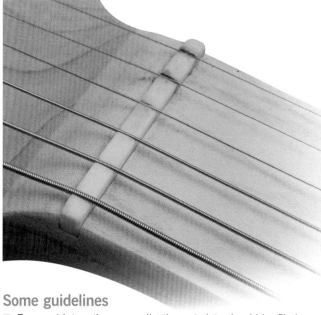

Some guidelines

- For good intonation generally, the nut slots should be filed at a back angle, putting the effective intonation fulcrum at the front of the slot nearest the frets. A little masking tape protects the headstock.

- The slots should be custom filed to your preferred string gauges – for which you'll need gauged nut files.
- Always allow more slot height on the wound 'bass' strings, as their thicker gauge requires more excursion.
- A feeler gauge can be set to equal the thickness of the string to fingerboard gap at the 2nd fret – assuming you're happy with this gap! Fit a capo at the 1st fret and see if the guitar feels better in this arrangement, then measure the gap.
- Use this measured feeler gauge depth plus a little extra to get you in the right area for nut slot height. The extra can act as a stop, to avoid filing too deep. Take it steady and keep checking with the strings up to tension. When it feels right, it is right.
- When the depth of the slots is in the right area, polish the slot with some gauged abrasive cord. Luthiers make their nut slots shiny smooth for optimum performance.
- Finish with a little graphite for lubrication.

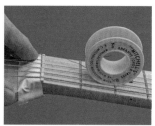

Compensated nuts

A 'compensated nut' is one that's been designed to improve note accuracy anywhere on the fretboard. I wasn't convinced about them until Brian May showed me how he'd compensated his zero fret – it works for him and deserves consideration!

Earvana actually manufacture these ready to go for most popular guitar types. In theory they compensate at the nut end of the string in a similar way that an adjustable saddle compensates for varying string gauges over the string length. They're particularly effective if you like to mix open strings and fretted notes in the first to fifth position.

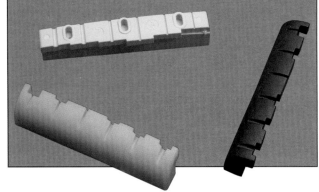

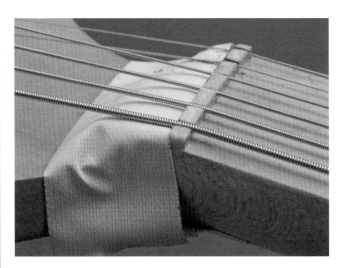

Nut adjustments on the guitars built for this book

The '50s 'S' type shown on page 138 is an interesting case for the nut accommodation. For authenticity I've strung this 012-056 – a common gauge for the '50s, but more associated these days with acoustic guitars – so I'm using a set of files matching those gauges.

I'm also allowing a lot more height at the bass strings to let those big boys move.

The treble, however, I'm able to drop a little lower. The key as always is to still follow the neck radius, which gives a great feel to the end result.

The flatter radius on our modern Alumitone guitar and the lighter gauge 009-042 strings means the basses are lower in the nut slots but not stifled. Remove a little from the top of the nut if necessary to free the bass strings, which only need to be two-thirds enclosed in the slot. I've positioned the first string away from the fingerboard edge specifically to allow for more finger vibrato potential, and adjusted the other strings to correspond with this. In the end set-up is about very specific playing styles. There's no one perfect set-up – it's whatever works for you!

I use different set-ups on different guitars – the '50s guitar set-up for '50s-style vibrato arm playing, and the modern guitar set-up for 'string bending' modern styles.

String height, string radius and intonation

The precise details of saddle designs vary, but the general principles remain the same whether the saddles are pressed steel or cast in brass. Fingerboard radii vary more than ever, so always check the fingerboard before adjusting saddles.

1 Check the current action height at the 17th fret with a feeler gauge. (This 'guitar specific' feeler gauge from Cruz Tools has a specific 'action orientated' .025in (.063mm) blade, which saves a bit of fiddling! If you need a higher action you can still add extra, slimmer blades.

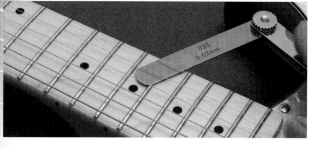

OR Measure the distance between the bottom of the strings and top of the 17th fret. In practice I find this little Corian wedge useful, as it's easier to use than a minuscule ruler! A pencil mark on the wedge can then be simply measured.

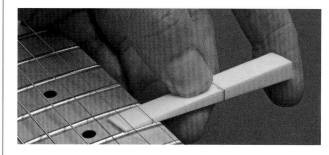

Always set the string heights and radius first and then adjust the string lengths for intonation, as raising or lowering the strings will affect the effective sounding length.

✏ Tech Tip

I find it best to set the first string height first, as this is often the most critical on an 'S' type. Set the first string high enough to avoid 'choking' when bending the string in the high fret positions. The other string heights should follow the neck radius pattern.

John Diggins – Luthier

---

2 Usually with a .050 Allen key, adjust the two pivot adjustment screws to achieve the desired overall string height for the first string at the 17th fret. A good guide height is ¹⁄₁₆in/.0625in on the classic 7.25in radius.

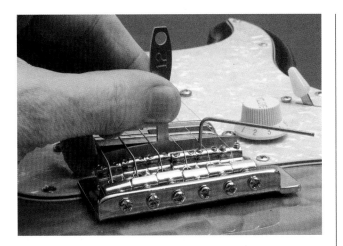

3 Adjust the sixth string bridge saddle to the 'vintage' ⁵⁄₆₄ in height according to the standard chart recommendations, then adjust the other bridge saddles to follow the neck radius as indicated by the appropriate under-string radius gauge. Retune the guitar.

These recommended action settings and radius measurements are, of course, only a guide. You can obviously experiment with the individual saddle height until your desired sound and feel is achieved.

NB: Adjusting string heights affects the effective sounding length of the string, and this naturally affects intonation, so you'll now need to adjust the string lengths.

✏ Tech Tip

It's worth checking the intonation at the 19th fret of the first string (B natural) against the open B string. If the open B and E are in tune then the 19th fret and open B shouldn't 'beat'. This applies equally to the 20th fret on the B string and the open G string. Similar checks should be tried on the 19th fret for all the other strings.

John Diggins – Luthier

---

1 Tune the open string to E concert. Check the harmonic note at the 12th fret of the first string as compared to the same fretted note. All the sounded notes should be precisely the same pitch though in different octaves. I use an extremely accurate electronic strobe tuner, which will visually display any discrepancy in 'cents', either 'flat' or 'sharp'.

NB: Take care to protect the guitar paintwork with a duster, taped in place with a low-adhesion masking tape.

2 If the string sounds or indicates 'flat' at the 12th fret when compared with the 12th harmonic, turn the longitudinal screw anticlockwise, thereby moving the saddle towards the neck. This usually requires a No '1' Phillips.

Adjust until the harmonic, open string and 12th fret all indicate or sound at the same pitch. Repeat this procedure for all six strings.

String trees lubricate and adjust

Introducing a round string guide to pull the first and second strings in towards the neck is the simplest solution to achieving enough break angle at the nut. The round string guide is a classic but is more often replaced by a seagull-wing string tree, which does the same job. You can experiment with the height of this by substituting or removing interchangeable fixing posts.

■ The slightest touch of lubrication (using Lipsalve, Vaseline or the Lubri-Kit syringe) will avoid any 'sticking' causing intonation problems. This particularly applies when heavy use is made of the vibrato/tremolo arm.

■ If necessary a second string tree can cover the third and fourth strings and is aesthetically a neater solution than a single or triple 'tree'.

■ A third option features a neat combination of a low friction 'roller'-type string tree for the first and second strings combined with staggered lower string posts for the top four strings. This is an effective solution to the 'nut tension' issue.

✎ Tech Tip

The extra string tree helps when a player replacing his strings doesn't allow enough windings on the string post, leaving a fairly gentle slope up to the nut – the string spacer provides the necessary pressure at the nut.

Andy Gibson

An alternative 'evolved' trem

The vintage model 'S' type trem has served guitarists well over the last 60 years. However, some guitarists prefer a more modern take on the 'knife edge' spring-balanced principle.

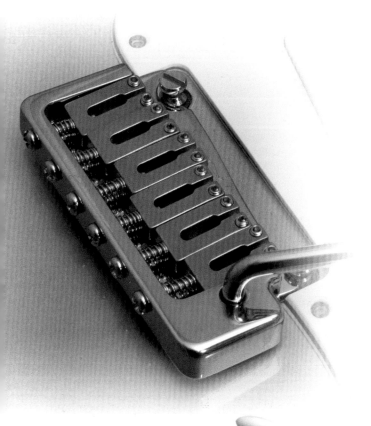

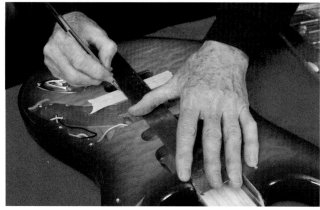

Ideally the 9.9mm cavities for these should be marked up and then drilled on a bench drill. The two posts then replace the two outer screws most often utilised on a vintage set-up.

All the rest of the installation follows the procedure for the vintage set-up shown on page 42.

The substantial mass of the all-steel block combined with the improved stability of the bridge posts and solid saddles is a useful design evolution.

This Wilkinson trem marries all the simplicity of the original with a modern two-point fixture and a solid steel trem block, as well as staggered string holes for easier access.

If you decide to go this route the only significant construction difference is the need for two bridge posts inserted into the top of the guitar.

Rattle and hum: screening issues

The earliest solid guitars needed very little screening – there were no mobile phones, radio taxis, fluorescent lights, computers or iPads etc. However, guitars of the '50s did have a small amount of screening around the control area, which I'm duplicating on our '50s 'S' type using self-adhesive screening foil.

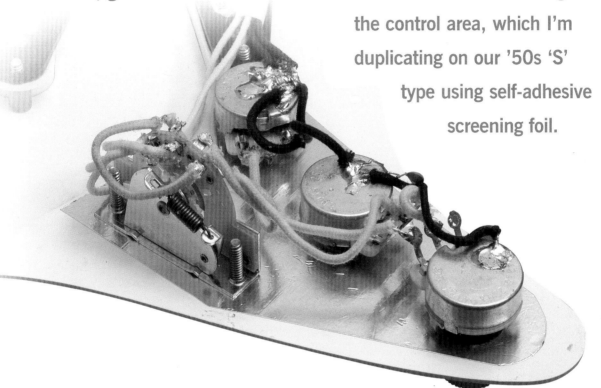

1 With the controls temporarily removed, press the foil into position with the backing paper intact. This should leave some guide impressions in the foil.

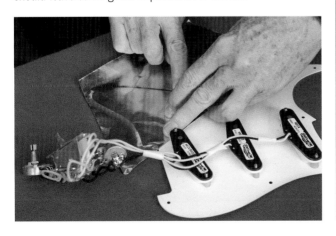

2 Cut along the guide impressions with scissors.

3 I used a printers' roller to smooth on the foil, avoiding air bubbles and simultaneously peeling off the backing paper.

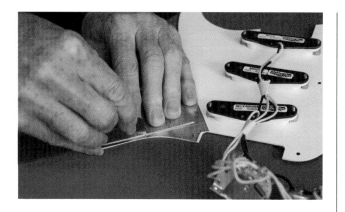

4 Trim the foil if necessary with a sharp craft knife...

5 ...and peel of any excess before the glue sets.

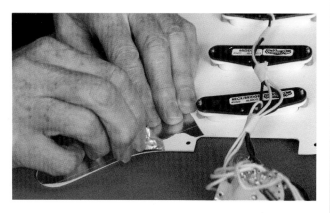

The finished 'period correct' '50s screening is fine if you're working in a home studio. However, on stage with modern lighting and radio interference it's worth applying a more comprehensive screening barrier.

Here we'll be using CuPro-Cote, a copper-based paint that gives a resistance measurement on wood of 1.2ohms per inch. The manufacturers claim to have achieved 43dB RF (radio frequency) suppression using this paint!

Safety first

Always use a vapour barrier facemask/respirator and eye protection when applying specialist paints.

1 Carefully remove the covers from all the cavities you intend to screen. Keep all the screws together in a series of pots and trays – it's worth labelling these now, as putting the wrong screws back in the wrong holes will inevitably cause problems.

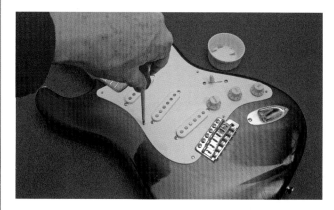

2 Carefully prepare the surfaces for painting. Using glass paper, remove any grease or rough woodwork that might hamper the adhesion of the paint.

3 Apply the first coat of screening paint and allow to dry.

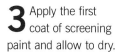

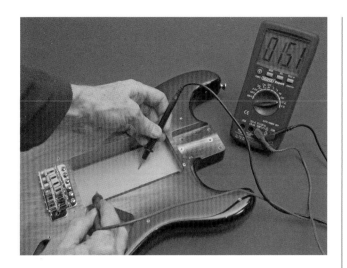

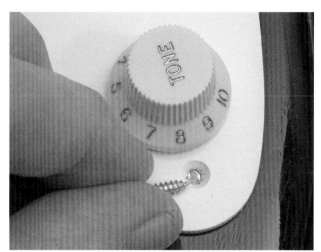

4 Apply a second coat of the screening paint. This second coat dramatically improves the effectiveness and continuity of the new screen. When the paint's dry, check for continuity of the 'circuit' created by your new screen. The easiest way to do this is by placing electronic multimeter prongs at several spaced points on the finish and seeing what continuity you've achieved.

5 If necessary solder a wire from your new screen to the earth side of your circuits. The need for this will depend on the extent of your painting and whether or not the paint is going to contact an existing earth point on reassembly. In this specific case a strip of self-adhesive copper connects the cavity screening to the pickguard screening.

6 The copper strip is cut to size...

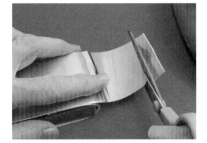

7 ...and self-adheres to the cavity.

8 With the pickguard in place good earth continuity is achieved via one of the pickguard screws.

9 Carefully reassemble the jack assembly, checking for all points of contact with the new screened surface. All live jack connections must be clear of contact with the new surface unless they're required to be 'grounded'. When re-soldering, a dab of 'tinner cleaner' RS561 533 will improve the conductivity of the solder iron heat and aid a quicker, more effective solder joint. Ensure the guitar finish is well protected from solder splashes.

■ The same procedure would be effective in all the control cavities. See the case study 'Red Special' on page 104 for some very comprehensive copper strip screening.

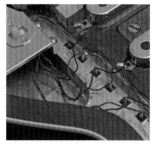
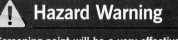

> ### ⚠ Hazard Warning
>
> **Screening paint will be a very effective conductor, so be careful to only apply it where a route to earth or ground is desirable. A bit of paint in the wrong place, which on reassembly touches a 'hot' wire, can short circuit the guitar.**

BUILD YOUR OWN ELECTRIC GUITAR

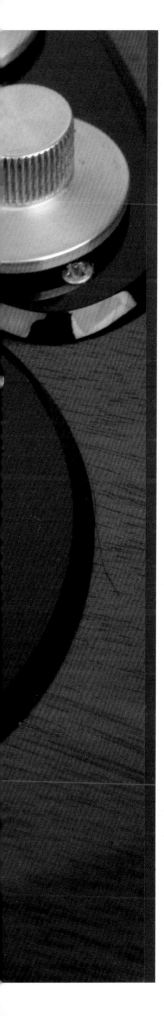

Case studies

Few professional guitarists choose to play a home-built guitar, though as a 'bitsa' – bits of this and bits of that – Eric Clapton's famous 'Blackie' comes close. It was assembled by Eric in the 1970s, and features on many of his classic recordings. The two pros most famous for their DIY skills are Brian May of Queen and Bo Diddley of the Rock and Roll Hall of Fame. Brian's guitar grew out of necessity, as the 'S' type played by his hero Hank Marvin was financially beyond the reach of a 16-year-old schoolboy. Bo Diddley just wanted to be noticed, and if the audience remembered 'the guy with the weird guitar' he was happy. Bo's guitar was initially less successful as an instrument than Brian's, so Gretsch came to the rescue. Brian's 'Red Special' has proved difficult to exactly replicate, though the latest limited edition by Andrew Guyton is so good that Brian plays one himself.

LEFT 'Under the hood' of the real Red Special.

RIGHT An unusual 'plectrum' – Brian May's 'sixpence'.

Brian May's 'Red Special'

Made in England
Serial No. none (the original) and
#050973 (the RSR 18 replica)

In August 1963, aged 16, schoolboy Brian May couldn't afford an 'S' type guitar so he and his engineer father Harold made their own. Constructed from recycled wood, home-acquired materials and partly carved with a schoolboy's penknife, this is now the iconic rock guitar that features on *Bohemian Rhapsody* and virtually all of Queen's hits.

Brian reckons 'The Fireplace', as he sometimes refers to the end product (for reasons that will become apparent), was an innovative instrument for its time – the first guitar he's aware of to be built with feedback as a goal rather than a nuisance. He wanted long, screaming sustain and for the guitar to sing along with him. May also figured out how to make his first pickups by winding thin wire on magnets and plugging these prototypes into his Dad's radio. Fortunately many '50s and '60s radios had a pickup input intended for amplifying a 78rpm record turntable stylus.

For our case study I examined Brian's original guitar at his Ascot home, and also one of the replicas identical to those he uses as backup, made by luthier Andrew Guyton. There have been many previous replica 'Red Specials' but these Guyton guitars are reckoned by Brian and his guitar tech Peter Malandrone to be the most accurate.

Condition on arrival

The 'Old Lady' – another of Brian's nicknames for his guitar – has seen a bit of action, while the Guyton replica is 'as new'. Curiously, in real life the original 'Red Special' is *brown*, but always photographs red!

General description

■ The guitar is a fascinating diversion – a twin cut 'semi-acoustic' with bolt-on neck and three pickups, all with series and out of phase connection potential.

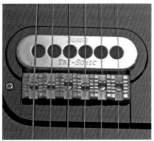

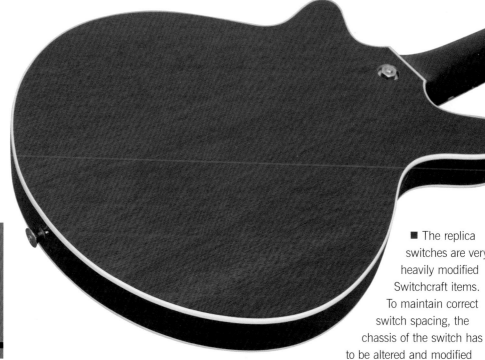

■ The volume and tone knobs are aluminium knobbed master volume and master tone; the volume (at the back) has a red indicator dot and both are secured with a 1.4mm Allen key to an unusual non-bolted pot post.

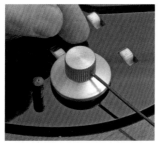

■ The PU switching is via six switches and offers any pickup combination either in or out of phase. The pickup switching allows any or all of the pickups to be 'summed' in series for a distinctive and unusual sound.

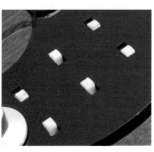

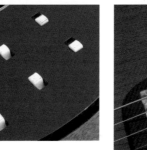

■ The replica switches are very heavily modified Switchcraft items. To maintain correct switch spacing, the chassis of the switch has to be altered and modified to accept new plates. The switch tips are then replaced with custom-machined items to replicate the size and feel of the originals. These are then mounted to an aluminium chassis plate that's shaped and fixed like the original guitar.

■ The original scratchplate has a star inlay which is just there to hide a hole once used to switch on an internal distortion unit (long since scrapped).

■ The replica pickups are Burns lookalike single coils.

■ The original rewound neck pickup and fingerboard has taken a battering from Brian's favourite pre-decimal British sixpenny piece 'plectrum'.

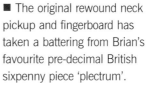

■ The original guitar has an aluminium bridge. The string roller saddles are adjustable to a certain extent for intonation. The replica is slightly more sophisticated, with more string length options.

■ The one-piece quarter-sawn Brazilian mahogany neck is even chunkier than a Fender 'boat' neck. One reason it's so thick is schoolboy Brian tired of carving it with a penknife! The replica is 24mm thick and maintains that profile with very little taper to the body. The scale length is a very short 24in. This creates a looser feel for the strings, which is ideal for Brian's extensive use of string bending and his wide vibrato. The width at the nut is 47mm. I have no doubt that this substantial neck is part of the sound of the 'Red Special'.

■ The side position markers include an interesting position 'V' marker.

■ The strings pass over a zero fret and through a worn Bakelite string guide. The replica is pristine with no wear.

■ The bolt-on neck is unusual in having one large bolt which sits beneath the fingerboard and goes through a hole in the body, where a nut is attached; it's also screwed down by two small wood screws at the tenon end, which ends just before the bridge pickup. The original is rusty, the replica is pristine.

■ The very slinky black-painted quarter-sawn oak fingerboard has 24 x 2.7mm frets. The simple mother-of-pearl button 'dot markers' are actual buttons on the original, with inlays at frets 1, 5, 9, 15, 17, 21 (one dot), 7 and 19 (two dots), and 12 and 24 (three dots).

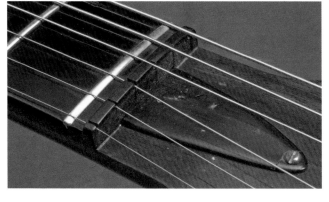

■ The neck pitch is 2° and the headstock angle 4° – not much, but the short scale and low tension strings make this work.

■ Brian recently glued a sixpence to the headstock of the original – this custom sixpence has his head as 'The Queen'!

■ The fingerboard radius is the classic 7.25in. This is matched at the saddles and the zero fret.

■ The stainless steel truss rod access is at the headstock, requiring a 2.5mm straight-slot for the one tiny wood screw, and a 9.5mm straight-slot for the rod nut itself.

■ The original machine heads have seen a few changes over 50 years, and the replica has adjustable Schaller back-locking tuners, fitted with modified Gotoh pearloid buttons. The locking tuners mean there are no string windings to unwind when using the trem.

■ The strings on this guitar are gold-plated Optima gold 'Brian May Custom Gauge' – .009, .011, .016, .024, .032 and .042.

■ The front of the replica headstock has Brian's signature.

■ The semi-solid body is made from oak, blockboard and mahogany veneer and has several large cavities and a central support batten. The guitar weighs a comfortable 8.25lb and the body thickness is a slim 39mm. The original has white shelf edging applied as binding. The body is finished in Rustins Plastic Coating.

■ The strap buttons on the original have Grolsch beer bottle rings as strap locks. These are cheap, simple and effective but increasingly difficult to obtain.

Trem

■ Removing one 6mm straight-slot screw gives lubrication access to the two springs.

■ The original tremolo system is made from an old hardened-steel knife-edge shaped into a V, with two motorbike valve springs to counter the string tension, all accurately reflected on the replica.

■ On the replica these rollers move beautifully and don't easily fall off – as sometimes happens with the original (the original arm itself was from a bicycle saddlebag, with one of Brian's Mum's plastic knitting needle tips looking suitably Fenderlike).

■ It's worth tightening the output jack retainer. This tends to work loose, causing crackles and intermittent output. A useful gadget for holding the internal jack still whilst tightening the outer nut is the 'Jack the Gripper' tool. You'll need a ½in socket wrench.

■ The trem arm is tightened 'Meccano'-style with an 8mm bike spanner, revealing its roots! The tension of the trem springs is adjustable by screwing the bolts – which run through the middle of the springs – in or out via two small access holes next to the rear strap button.

■ To reduce friction, the bridge was completed with rollers to allow the strings to return perfectly in tune after using the tremolo arm.

Shawn Leaver

The current owner of this replica is Shawn Leaver, a 'Red Special' enthusiast who has had the pleasure of playing Brian's original and this replica next to each other, and felt they were identical – though his is in better condition! 'I've owned pretty much every other replica ever made and they've always had little problems. I had a Japanese replica and the neck was a little bit too flat on that, and it had larger switches. I went through three different sets of pickups with the guitar, trying to get it sound closer to how I thought the original would sound. But I've had the Guyton for a couple of years now and I've never had to modify it. I'm completely happy with it. I'll be buried with that guitar!'

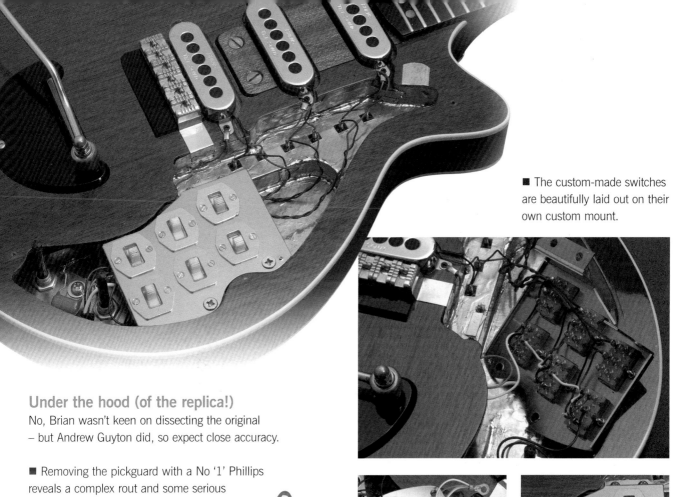

■ The custom-made switches are beautifully laid out on their own custom mount.

Under the hood (of the replica!)
No, Brian wasn't keen on dissecting the original – but Andrew Guyton did, so expect close accuracy.

■ Removing the pickguard with a No '1' Phillips reveals a complex rout and some serious one-off engineering. The pickguard is fully copper-screened.

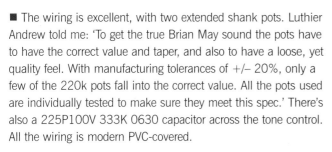

■ Everything is immaculately copper screened and methodically wired – only an engineer would do this! These copper-tape connectors meet the back of the screened pickguard on assembly, forming a perfect ground cage around the switches.

■ The wiring is excellent, with two extended shank pots. Luthier Andrew told me: 'To get the true Brian May sound the pots have to have the correct value and taper, and also to have a loose, yet quality feel. With manufacturing tolerances of +/– 20%, only a few of the 220k pots fall into the correct value. All the pots used are individually tested to make sure they meet this spec.' There's also a 225P100V 333K 0630 capacitor across the tone control. All the wiring is modern PVC-covered.

Dr Brian May

Dr Brian May CBE PhD Astrophysics (born 19 July 1947 in London), son of Harold and Ruth May, attended Hampton Grammar School, where he formed his first band, Nineteen Eighty-Four (named after George Orwell's novel). He left school with ten GCE 'O' Levels and three 'A' levels, in Physics, Mathematics and Applied Mathematics. He studied Mathematics and Physics at Imperial College, London, and graduated with a BSc degree with honours.

Brian May with the author.

■ Incidentally, a lot of the machine screws are Pozidrivs – unusual on guitars – which follow the historic Phillips format. Brian had originally purchased a set of Burns Tri-Sonic pickups but rewound them with reverse wound/reverse polarity, and 'potted' the coils with Araldite epoxy to reduce microphonics. Previously he'd wound his own pickups, but he didn't like the resulting sound because of their conventional polarity, alternating north–south instead of all north.

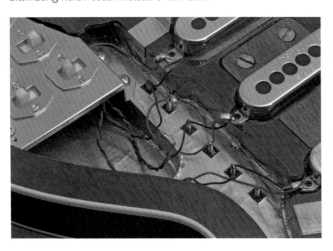

■ These three replicas are series-wired single-coil pickups which, like the originals, have non-adjustable pole pieces and utilise wooden shims for fixing their overall height from the body. The neck and middle have no shims but some fibre spacer washers in the fixing screws. The bridge pickup does have a wooden shim.

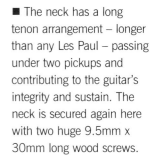

■ The neck has a long tenon arrangement – longer than any Les Paul – passing under two pickups and contributing to the guitar's integrity and sustain. The neck is secured again here with two huge 9.5mm x 30mm long wood screws.

■ The neck is further secured with a 13mm nut.

■ The tenon is beautifully snug, and has the weirdest truss rod end secured to the neck bolt!

Pedal power

Brian uses up to 14 VOX AC30TBX, top-boost version amps with Blue Alnico speakers, an idea he picked up from Rory Gallagher.

Guitar tech Peter Malandrone customises Brian's amps by removing the circuitry for the brilliant and vib-trem channels (leaving only the circuitry for the normal), and this alters the tone slightly, with a gain addition of 6–7dB. He always used a treble booster which, along with the AC30 and his custom 'Deaky' transistor amp, as built by Queen bass player John Deacon, went a long way in helping to create many of his signature guitar tones. He used the Dallas Rangemaster made famous by Eric Clapton for the first Queen albums.

Effects specialist Pete Cornish then built for him the TB-83 (32dB of gain), and that was used for all the remaining Queen albums. (That's Brian's cabling and labelling and Shawn's pedal). He switched in 2000 to the Fryer's booster, which gives less boost than the TB-83 but a different EQ curve.

Live, he wires some amps with only guitar and others with all effects returns such as delay, flanger and chorus. He often has a bank of 14 AC30s, which are grouped as normal, chorus, delay 1 and delay 2. On his pedal board he has a switch unit made by Cornish and modified by Fryer that allows him to choose which amps are active. He has also used a Foxx Foot Phaser, notably on *We Will Rock You*.

I see a little silhouetto of a man,
Scaramouche, Scaramouche, will you do the Fandango?

Signed off

This guitar has a very distinctive character. With very light gauge strings, a sixpenny-piece pick, out of phase and very loud, it is a very sensitive and expressive instrument. This one knew how to play *The National Anthem* in both octaves and self-introduced pinched harmonics! You'll need at least four VOX AC30s wired in parallel to fill Wembley. Six other empty boxes would look extra cool.

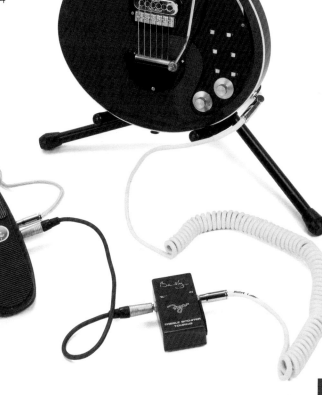

Brian May on the 'Red Special'

As Brian May is the maker of the most successful home-built guitar in the world I thought it would be useful to ask him about the thinking behind his guitar the 'Red Special'.

At his home in England, next to his observatory, and in a store full of Red Specials, Brian started by telling me about his first guitar.

"I still it have it! I built pickups for it and it's been recently refinished by Andrew Guyton. It's an Egmond Toledo acoustic – it's exactly like the one George Harrison had – a piece of crap! It was given to me for my seventh birthday, and it seemed huge at the time, as I was so small.

I made a pickup to for it, figuring that if you wiggled steel strings in front of a magnet it would make a current. I put some magnets on a plastic base, wound loads of wire round them, connected them up to my Dad's radio, and it worked! (Author's note: Many '50s and '60s radios had a 'pickup input' intended for amplifying a 78 RPM record turntable stylus.)

■ Given how well the Red Special turned out, especially for a 16-year-old working with his Dad, I asked Brian how far he had got as a player before building it.

"Quite a long way really! It's amazing how quickly you develop. I'm not a great technician, I'm not a virtuoso, but most of what I do now I could probably just about do when I was certainly 18 or so. I think what changes most is what you're saying with your playing.

The guitar was an experiment really, and my Dad was quite a brilliant man, he could turn his hand to anything – electronics, metalwork, woodwork – he had an amazing instinct for things, and he taught me some of that stuff.

I knew what I wanted! I'd played around with my friends' guitars – they had things like Hofner's, imitation Stratocasters and Watkins Rapiers – so I saw their faults and I thought, 'well I can make something better than that together with my Dad'. So we did a lot of experiments. We got a big piece of wood and stretched some strings across it and tried out various tremolo devices, just to see what happened mechanically.

A tremolo is quite an important device really – not something you'd have as standard on guitars in those days. A lot of people had problems with trems that wouldn't return to pitch, so I tried to eliminate friction by coming straight through here at the headstock, which is almost parallel, with a zero fret that the strings rest on, and almost no sideways friction.

The idea for the zero fret actually came from my old Egmond guitar. I knew you needed enough pressure, but not too much pressure, here in order to keep the intonation. I was able to separate the 'sideways' from the 'up-and-down' by doing that. I didn't want the strings resting on the bottom, on a bit of plastic. This way your zero fret is the same as your 1st fret, so should sound the same. Then we tried to eliminate friction at the bridge by putting little rollers on the saddles – it was all invention!"

■ I asked if Brian had seen a Bigsby by then.

"There were Bigsby trems around, but they didn't have roller bridges, they had a big sort of barrel thing. I think Bigsby may have introduced rollers later, but I don't think anyone had ever done this before. I carved it all out myself from a solid hunk of aluminium, and sawed all the slots out, then polished it all up and cut it into six pieces. We had lots of hand tools, but no power tools. So the rollers I made myself by putting a drill in a vice and turning it, and filing away. Usually I got to the very end and slipped, and it would break, and I'd have to start again! Much later I got someone else to make them!"

■ I asked about the fabulous action on the Red Special – did Brian have that from the start?

"Yep, I wanted it to be easy. The Hofners and Egmond were difficult to play. I sawed the bridge down on the Egmond to make the action lower. I wanted the Special' to be nice and easy to play."

■ I asked Brian if it is true that he carved the neck with a penknife.

"Not just a penknife – we had planes and chisels and sandpaper. I think a penknife was used round here (near the nut), and the neck was a piece of a fireplace."

■ I asked what prompted Brian to install 'in-' or 'out-of-phase' switching, as that was very sophisticated for 1963.

"Well, I hooked the unassembled guitar up to my Dad's radio, as I'd done with the Egmond, and I had all the wires hanging out and I thought, 'well what do I do'? And I discovered that if I hooked the pickups up in series I got different kinds of sounds, and when I connected them in parallel I got another different set of sounds. Then I discovered that if I turned one of them round, the pick-ups would sort of fight against one another and you got yet another different kind of sound. I don't think anyone had ever done this, and I thought 'what a waste', if you can get all these different sounds, but you can't actually summon them up when you're playing. So I came up with an 'on' and 'off' for each pickup and a phase reversal for each pickup, and wired them all in series. I made the choice that they should all be in series and not in parallel because the sound was a bit warmer.

The bridge and mid fighting against each other, 'out of phase', gave very harsh harmonics, which is the *Bohemian Rhapsody* solo. The mid and neck together sound like a warm humbucker, because they're working together – again, if you turn them out of phase you get a very different sound. Much later there was a guy at Fender who liked the 'Special', and he made a Fender that had this switching system, but I don't think it ever became a commercial thing.

You have to learn the switching; not everyone finds it easy to begin with, but once you get the hang of it, that gives you a huge amount of control. It can sound like anything from an ES 335 to a Les Paul.

It's a very personal instrument. The buttons used for position markers and the knitting-needle tip came from my Mum, and the saddle-bag arm is off my bike. We built it because we couldn't afford a real one, and also it would be something no-one else had. It's the first guitar I'm aware of to be built with feedback as a goal rather than a nuisance. I wanted long, screaming sustain, and for the guitar to sing along with me."

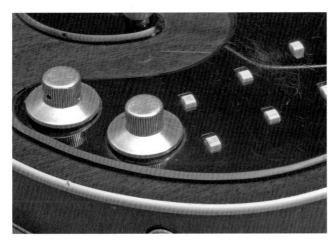

Pete Malandrone
– a guitar tech's perspective

I spent some time with Brian May's guitar tech Peter Malandrone and several 'Red Specials' including 'The Old Lady'.

■ I asked Pete what he felt made the 'Special' unique.

"Everything's unique. The neck is a mahogany bit from an old fireplace, some of it carved by hand by Brian. The main skeleton of the guitar is of oak block-board – an old neighbour's oak table, and all covered with two skins of mahogany veneer. It has shelf edging to hold it all together. It has a big acoustic pocket at the top, and one at the back underneath the scratchplate. Originally, Brian tells me, the guitar was going to have an f-hole.

The guitar also has a truss rod, but I can't imagine the neck would move! It's never been tightened or loosened. The rod looks like a piece of metal they just had lying around.

What makes it so nice is some of the normal household bits on it; filed down pearl buttons from mum's sewing box, a trem arm fashioned from an old bicycle saddle bag; the end of the trem – the knob – from one of his Mum's knitting needles! The trem springs are fashioned from old motorcycle valves springs.

The guitar remains mostly original, but the machine heads have been changed for locking ones. The control knobs are mild steel, and the brass bits were braised on a gas stove. It's a real home-made bit of art. His Dad also made a TV and a telescope, as they could not afford to buy these items."

■ I asked Pete about the pickups.

"They wound their own pick-ups, having bought a set of three, for six guineas, that Brian wasn't happy with. The replacements were quite microphonic, so they potted them – filled them up with Araldite. If they ever go wrong they are history – nobody is sure what happens to Araldite after 50 years! Again, that's kind of a happy accident! Given a choice, they may well have picked something else.

The strap locks are old Grolsch beer-bottle rubber gaskets – simple but effective."

Brian told Pete that the neck is as thick as it is, as he couldn't bring himself to whittle any more!

Andrew Guyton
– a luthier's perspective

I caught up with Andrew Guyton at his Suffolk workshop. Andrew now makes replicas of the 'Special' for Brian's stage use. Andrew has recently made a limited edition of 50 replica 'Specials'.

■ I first asked Andrew about the problems arising when replicating such a unique one off.

"The biggest difficulty was parts supply and recreating everything, because everything on the guitar is bespoke, and you have to do it the same way. The construction of the body is so complex. You've got to incorporate the layers, inserts etc. It's just designed to hold air, and keep the thing moving and feeling alive at stage volumes. Being hollow lends a tendency for acoustic feedback – air in there will move, and it's part of the design to encourage musical feedback.

The most difficult aspect of the trem was measuring the original, because I couldn't take it out of the guitar. So getting the fulcrum and pivot points right, with the bolts and knife edge, and getting the whole thing so that it would feel right, was difficult. But once you've got the measurements, it's just finding the actual engineer to make them. Rather than 'Mum's knitting needle' I used an adaptation of Fender Strat trem-arm tips just slightly reshaped.

The fretwire may be 'stock', but everything else is just made for that guitar. The current tuners are a mixture of 'Schaller' mechanics and 'Gotoh' buttons. But even these have to be altered to fit the 'Schallers' – nothing's easy on it! It's a history piece really – of its time… In 1964 you could just go into Radio Spares and buy some of this stuff, like the switches. Now the only real option you've got is Switchcraft, but their switch bodies are too long – the actuators are too big – to get the right spacing. You actually have to cut down the metal chassis of the switch, and then we bond a lot of aluminium plate on top of that, and then install white plastic actuators. It's all part of the aesthetics – you don't actually benefit in any way – it's just got to look and feel the same. They look similar; once the plate is off they're going to be similar. For 50 guitars it's difficult. For one maybe, but for 50!

I made Brian a version with a scalloped fingerboard, and that illustrated to me the difference that small things can made to the guitar. It's such a sensitive guitar, even with the adjustment of string gauges. For the scalloped one I just took 0.5mm–0.75mm out of the frets, and it sounded more like an SG! It gave it more of a 'Gibson-like' bark – just sounded a bit more aggressive.

The very long neck tenon probably does contribute to the sound, and probably so does the way it's fixed. The idea of having 2 screws and a bolt makes it very stable, and if you try and adjust the neck angle with shimming, the sound will just disappear – it's

got to have that contact from one end to the other. The whole thing has just got to be mated solid. If you've got any air in between, it just doesn't work."

■ I asked Andrew what he would change if he could.

"The truss rod and how the electrics are mounted, because if you change anything else it would start to lose its sound or change the sound. It would be more like a 'Brian May Special' (alluding to a Gibson SG Special?) – the mid-range. They are all Mahogany, not solid, but made of a Mahogany body and neck with ebony fingerboard. So it is going to sound different."

■ I asked about the short scale.

"I think it was just an ease thing – 24 frets, 24 inches, it was just an easy thing to do".

Shawn Leaver, who owns an Andrew Guyton replica, interjected here: "The scale was copied from a Burns guitar – Brian has been asked that before. Same with the position markers – he didn't think they were informative enough on the standard Strat, and the 24 frets is just a neat double octave"

Shawn continued: "I think it comes down to the fact that Andrew's the only guy that I know of that does the bridge mounted in the correct way, and the truss-rod bolt in the correct way, because when you turn the bolt nut on the back of the guitar to do the neck up, you can hear it vibrate along the entire guitar, and I think that contributes to how they sound. So if you go to that level of detail… It works!"

Andrew has recently offered Brian a doubleneck Red Special with 6- and 12-string necks. After some initial doubt, Brian has since taken the guitar out on tour!

Bo Diddley
'Electromatic' G5810

Made in China
Serial No. CYG11120981

The 'cigar-box guitar' concept dates back to the American Civil War period, when small Figaro brand cigar boxes were used to fashion fiddles, banjos and guitars. The modern fully functional 'artwork' example pictured left is by Tom Bingham of Corby, England, and is really a radical modification of an existing six-string guitar.

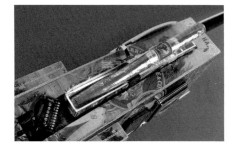

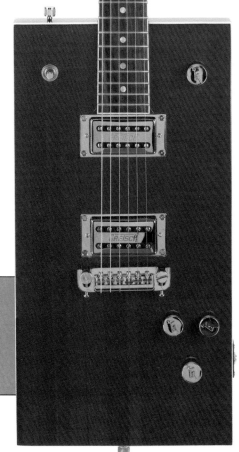

Jimi Hendrix started on a cigar-box guitar with rubber bands for strings, as did Carl Perkins and many others. Bo Diddley had a reputation for designing outlandish guitars, and he may have been inspired by cigar-box guitars he saw in Mississippi.

'The first one I had was called the "Cadillac tail",' he said. 'I was into the rocket-tail '59 Cadillac. I built that one myself. I also built the first square guitar – took the neck and electrics of a Gretsch, but that one got stolen. After that I got Gretsch to make them for me at their factory in Brooklyn.'

Condition on arrival

This Electromatic has seen a few knocks in transit but still works well despite that, and has a very distinctive sound, especially hooked up to a valve amp with a pulsing tremolo.

General description

■ The guitar is a practical combination of authentic Gretsch electrics with a radically simple square, solid body.

■ The volume and tone knobs are chromed metal with the 'G' logo and arrow, and include a separate master volume control on the front lower bout.

■ The three-way PU switch is also chromed and works bridge/both/neck.

■ The guitar has an interesting stop-tail bridge. This requires a 12mm straight-slot for two-point height adjustment. The basic two-point string length adjustment requires a No '1' Phillips, but each saddle can also be individually adjusted with a 4mm straight-slot.

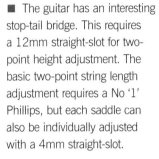

■ The two-piece maple neck has a joint at the 2nd fret and follows a typical 1960s 'C' profile with a constant taper to the body. The scale length is 25.5in and the width at the nut 43mm.

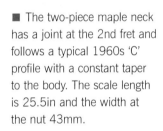

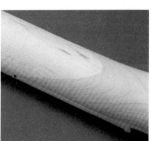

■ The pickups are Gretsch humbuckers.

■ The semi-solid body is two 240mm x 450mm rectangles of timber with several large cavities and a central support batten. The guitar weighs a comfortable 7.75lb and the body thickness is a consistent 1.75in – that's a 6in ruler disappearing under the pickups.

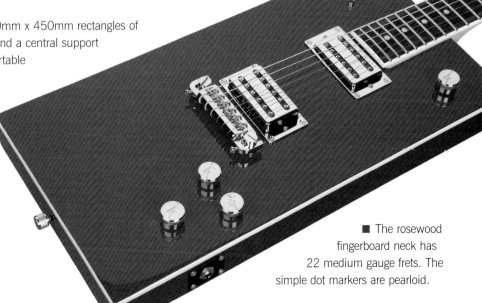

■ The rosewood fingerboard neck has 22 medium gauge frets. The simple dot markers are pearloid.

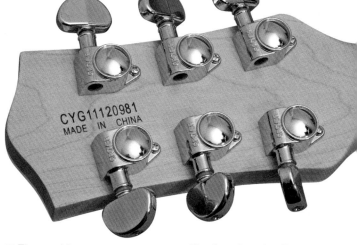

■ The signed truss rod access is at the headstock, requiring a 5mm Allen key.

■ The frcts are 2.89mm gauge and the nut is a piece of white plastic.

■ The machine heads are modern Grovers.

■ The fingerboard radius is a modern 12in. This is matched at the saddles.

■ The strings on this guitar are 009-046. When changing strings it's worth checking the machine head fixing screws, which tend to work loose. On the Diddley this requires a No '1' Phillips. Do not over-tighten – just enough to stop the machine head moving in normal use.

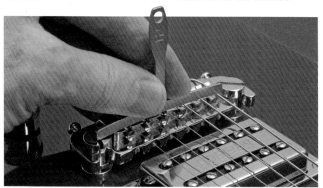

■ The knurled Gretsch strap buttons are very stylish, and the tops screw off to lock the strap in position.

Bo Diddley

Born Ellas Otha Bates in McComb, Mississippi, on 30 December 1928, Bo Diddley was an American singer, guitarist and songwriter who played a key part in the metamorphosis of blues music into rock'n'roll. His crazy guitars, distinctive Bo Diddley beat and charismatic persona made him a legend. He died in June 2008.

■ Whilst you have the tools out it's worth tightening the output jack retainer. This tends to work loose, causing crackles and intermittent output. Tightening entails a 12mm socket and a No '1' Phillips for the plate. A useful gadget for holding the jack still whilst tightening is the 'Jack the Gripper'.

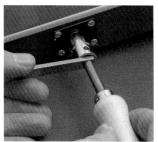

Under the hood

■ Removing one of the three rear panels using the usual No '1' Phillips driver reveals a clean rout.

■ The wiring is OK, with three tiny 500K pots and a capacitor routed to a modern fairly sturdy three-way switch and the master volume – which have their own access hatches. All the wiring is modern PVC-covered.

■ There's no electrical screening at present and it would be worth giving the cavities a coat of screened and earthed paint.

■ If loose the interesting volume and tone pots require a 2mm Allen key to tighten the knob and an 11mm socket to fix the pot itself.

■ The neck has no shims but several factory numbers.

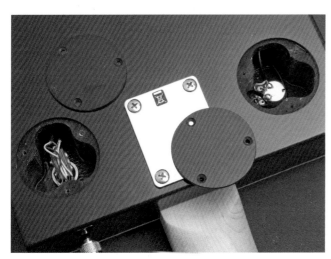

■ The two modern humbucking pickups have adjustable pole pieces that require a 3mm screwdriver and a No '0' Phillips for fixing their overall height from the body.

Signed off

This guitar needs a bit of repair work as the fingerboard is currently loose from the neck and there are a few cracks and dings in the lacquer, but it will be fine after a little TLC. Never trust a courier service with a guitar!

Constructing a cigar-box guitar

Though seemingly simple and unsophisticated the cigar box guitar lets us cheaply engage with all the key principles of guitar construction. This helps our understanding of important factors such as scale length, fret mark precision, the function of the nut, bridge and tuner placement, and stability and break angles, and perhaps even a basic understanding of guitar electronics at their simplest level.

Most CBG builders tend to simplify their instruments' courses to two or three strings – this also aids the understanding of guitar tunings, and perhaps why we've evolved to the very sophisticated modal stringing and tuning of the standard six strings.

What I really admire about the cigar-box approach is how it enables many people who (like me) perhaps feel overwhelmed by the luthier approach to building, to at least make a start.

It also encourages a creative and 'can do' approach to music-making itself, which can also tend to be overwhelmed by the mystique of the conservatoire. Many CBG players seem to invent their own tunings, playing styles and techniques, and this is healthy and liberating.

You'll need:

- A cigar box – or similar wooden box of large enough dimensions. I'm using a 9in x 8in 'Romeo and Juliet' box from importers cgarsltd.co.uk.
- A piece of hardwood timber for a neck.
- A fret template – an existing guitar will do.
- Some sort of bridge and nut materials.
- A pickup and output jack socket (optional).
- A set of tuners.
- Basic carpentry skills.

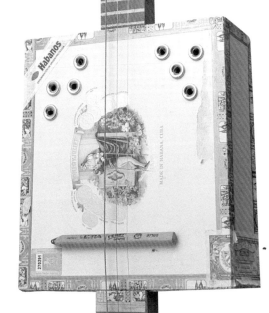

1 Choose a piece of neck timber to shape up a neck. A 3ft long 2 x 1in piece of hardwood will do the job – regular deal or pine will tend to warp easily under string pressure.

I could only get a small cigar box, so to balance things up I'm using a 1 x 1.75in piece of sapele found in the timber bin at my local carpenters' shop. This could have been used for a ukulele neck or an mbira body or even a Cadillac interior, and has a similar appearance to mahogany.

2 Square a line 6in in from one end of the timber as the nut position.

3 Measure 25.5in from there to establish the bridge position, and mark that up.

4 Lay the neck timber on the box with a suitable overhang – you want the bridge position about a third of an inch from the end of the box. Mark the neck.

5 Mark the neck position on the box itself. Establish a centre line and mark up the necessary cut-outs. The neck itself gives you the correct depth.

6 Cut out the neck slots in the cigar box. You're aiming for a snug fit, so cut on the 'waste' side of the line. A craft knife is less likely to tear the cigar box paper lining. You may want to reduce the neck timber to accommodate the lid of the box, if you want the neck flush with the body, though this isn't totally necessary on a higher action bottleneck guitar.

7 We definitely need to reduce the timber at the headstock to give some 'break angle' at the nut, reducing the timber by about one-third. The 'nut' height is a good guide, the 'nut' in this case being an old discarded bolt!

8 Mark up the timber to be removed.

9 Cut the 'nut line' with a tenon saw.

10 Saw away the major waste with a fret saw...

11 ...and chisel and rasp away any excess. This isn't easy going, as sapele is a good, hard wood!

12 These Microplane tools are great for some elementary shaping.

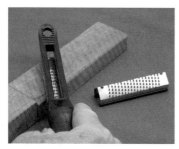

13 You could also do some cosmetic shaping of the headstock – perhaps draw round an aerosol lid? I'm just going to glue on a bit of cigar-box trimming.

14 You could also comfort-shape the edges off the back of the neck with a spoke shave and then use the Microplane for finer finishing before finally 'polishing' with glass paper.

15 Copy the fretting lines from a 25.5in scale-length guitar on to your CBG neck. I'm using a Stewmac fret polishing mask and a gold pen. This is the deluxe model!

16 Mark up, drill out and fit some tuners and bushings to the headstock.

17 Drill some holes for the tailpiece string access. You could line these with some kind of bushing or eyelet if you have anything suitable, otherwise a simple washer will prevent string slippage.

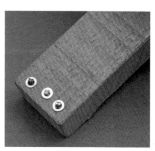

18 Site some soundholes in the box top away from the playing area. Brass curtain eyelets cover the crude holes.

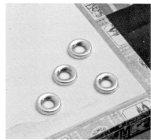

19 Reinforce the box by gluing and clamping some scrap wood battens inside and under the neck. Nice firm joints at the neck connections will help generate some coupling for smoking tone. Use some scrap wood to protect the exterior of the box from the clamps.

20 Fit the neck and glue to the battens. Before fixing the top consider adding a magnetic or piezo pickup if you have one and need one. (I'm retro-fitting, which is harder!)

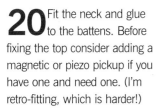

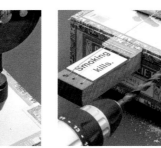

21 I'm trying an inexpensive Artec guitar piezo under the 'pencil' bridge. I drilled a 3.5mm hole for the piezo cable and will also need a 10mm jack socket hole. I initially plan to try using an external preamp, though onboard jack socket preamps are also easily obtained.

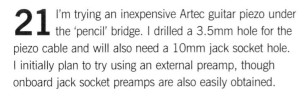

22 Glue and clamp down the soundboard/lid.

23 Fit a discarded bolt for a nut. As I'm designing this CBG for bottleneck blues I'm shimming the nut high with a lollipop stick.

24 String up the guitar. I'm going for an open 5th and octave tuning EBE – this works fine for simple slide blues. Then fix something for a bridge. This pencil came to hand. Check it's at the 25.5in mark.

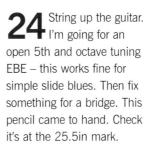

25 MAS JUN07 – a rare post-CBS model!

26 Self-adhesive stationers' dots help you find your way around the neck. Choose yourself a bottleneck slide and Kerrang!

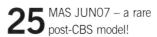

Signed off

Engaging with the cigar-box guitar has great potential. As well as practical involvement with the mechanics of 'what makes a guitar tick' there's also a musical element, encouraging us to unpick the sophistication of standard tuning and string-to-string intervals and to think about scales, modes and chords in a more aware and potentially creative way, analysing what a guitar is made of and promoting thought regarding what music itself is 'made' of. All for the price of a cigar box and some scrap timber.

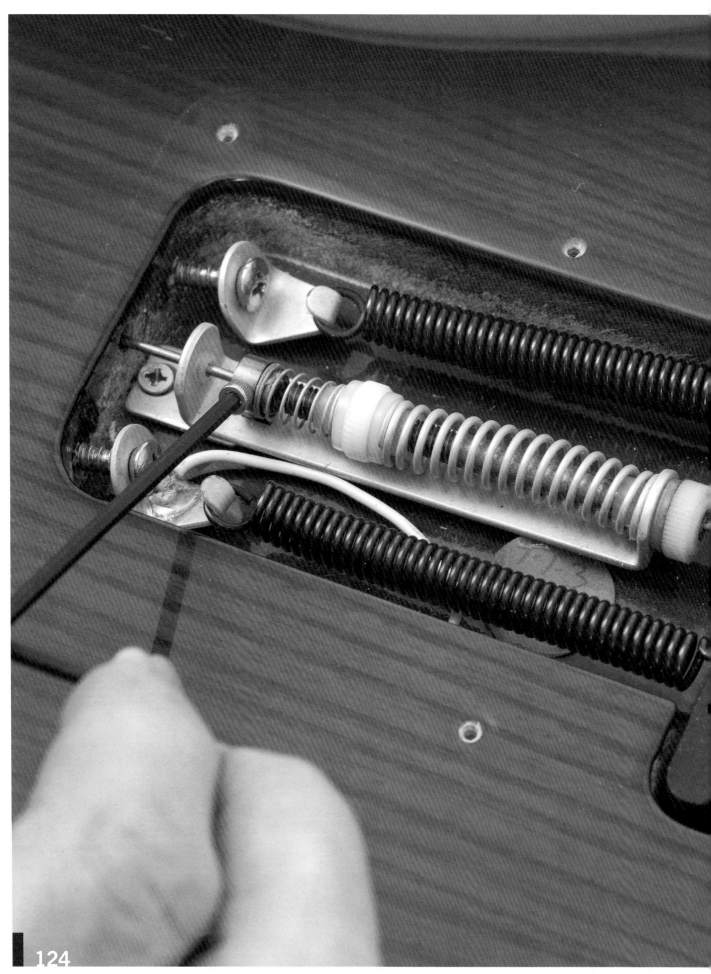

BUILD YOUR OWN ELECTRIC GUITAR

Optional extras

Having constructed and set up your own 'S' type there are a few extras you may want to consider alongside the continuing options for upgrades on pickups and hardware. I've found the Tremsetter useful – though it's not perfect for all playing styles, so I confine it to one guitar. The hard tail blocked-off trem option is also worth considering if you don't need a trem – this is Eric Clapton's standard set-up. Many guitarists also like their guitars to look 'lived in', so a little light relic work might be in order.

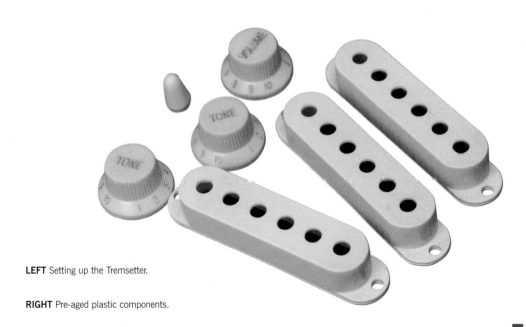

LEFT Setting up the Tremsetter.

RIGHT Pre-aged plastic components.

Hard-tail conversion

If you're not a trem/vibrato user you may want to block off the trem but retain the springs and metal trem block, as they all contribute to an 'S' type's distinctive sound.

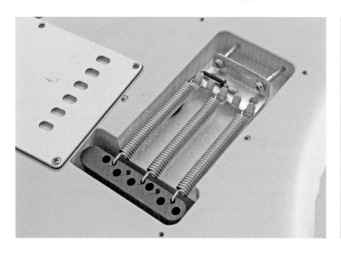

Tech Tip

Three springs in parallel will be fine for 009–046-gauge strings. If you are using heavy-gauge 012–056, then you will need five, as designed. When the trem is 'blocked off' you may as well have the benefit of five.

Frank Marvel

1 Remove the strings (one at a time and working from the outer two inwards, ie first and sixth, then second and fifth – this will avoid putting the guitar neck through any sudden changes in tension and will mean less resetting).

2 Carefully remove the plastic backplate from the tremolo/vibrato cavity using a No '1' Phillips screwdriver.

3 Carefully measure the cavity behind the block – a vernier gauge is ideal for this.

4 From a small scrap of hardwood or ply, fashion a custom block to fit the tapers inside the cavity behind the existing metal tremolo block. These Microplane tools are perfect for wood shaping, but a rasp will do the job at a pinch. The block will be approximately ½in/12mm thick by 3in/75mm long by as much as 1¾in/40mm deep, though you should rough-cut it slightly oversize and then custom sand it for a snug fit. This example is actually quite small but effective.

5 With the trem springs as a grip the new ply block should hold itself snugly in position.

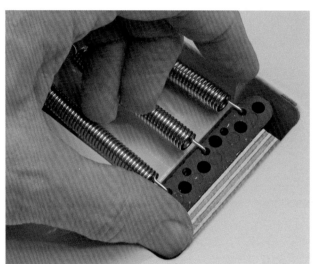

6 At least one of the trem springs should be left in place, as this provides earth or ground continuity via the wiring to the spring 'claw'. As they contribute to the sound they're best all left in place – Eric Clapton has five in the back of his hard-tail.

7 Replace the plastic tremolo coverplate. You may want to consider replacing the cover with the latest type. This has larger access holes for stringing, and the metal vibrato block may now be otherwise difficult to access in its new 'blocked off' position.

Tremsetter option

Some players find the 'wobble' associated with a floating trem – as well as the tendency for *all* the strings to change tension and pitch when one string is 'bent' up in pitch – disturbing. The Tremsetter may be the answer. This adjustable stabilising spring returns the trem more precisely to rest following use. Note the split trem claw and the need for a special 'bent' Phillips No '1' screwdriver (though you can remove the Tremsetter spring at a pinch).

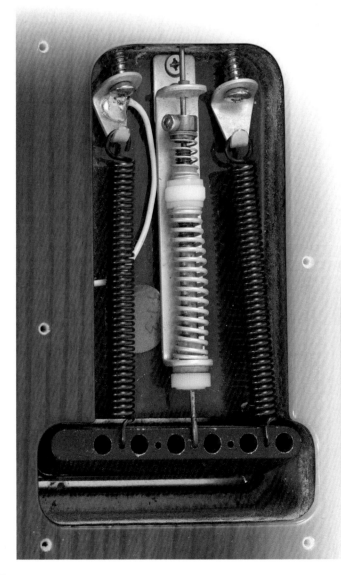

On a gigging guitar the Tremsetter may have specific advantages, especially if you use a lot of string bending. The device's stabilising effect means the bridge is less inclined to move during string bending and palm muting and this may work for your style of playing.

It's important that all the components of the Tremsetter are securely fixed and the tension adjusted to balance the 'return' position.

I've personally tried a Tremsetter over a one-year period and feel that whilst it changes the 'feel' of the classic trem it has advantages for certain guitars. I wouldn't want it on my '57, but for a versatile gigging guitar it's very useful.

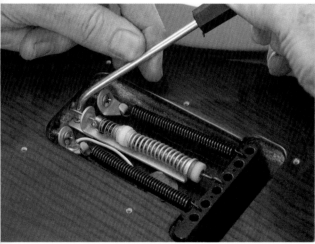

■ For more detailed installation instructions an excellent video demonstration by the Tremsetter's inventor, David Borisoff, can be found at www.hipshotproducts.com.

Installation

The Tremsetter can be installed as a retrofit on any trem-equipped 'S' type. The istallation requires:

1 Replacing the single claw with two split claws...

2 ...drilling two small holes in the guitar body...

3 ...and attaching a plate to the bottom of the trem cavity – not ideal on a vintage collectors' piece, but fine on your custom special.

4 The hole at the back of the trem cavity enables the Tremsetter guide pin to move freely.

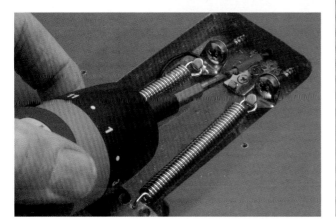

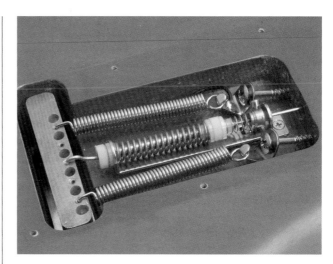

Adjusting

The installed Tremsetter is widely adjustable. The precise setting will depend on:

- The gauge of strings.

- How you want the trem to 'feel'.

- The torsion of your original trem springs.

Experiment until you achieve something that works for you.

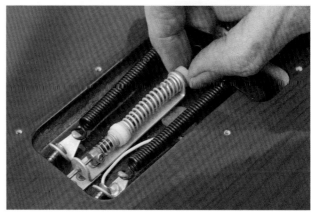

A little light relic work

If you prefer your guitars to look and feel 'played in' but don't want to pay for the privilege then you may consider a little DIY. What's required is a little speeded up distress – applying the effects of 40 years of wear and tear in a day. In this instance we'll be looking at a Biffy Clyro 'S' type that I've recently distressed, but the techniques used would work just as well on our 'newly constructed' guitars.

Tech Tip
My own approach to relic work is to encourage the simulation of oxidation and rust , as well as 'plastic fading', but to largely leave 'dings' to natural occurence rather than simulation.
Frank Marvel

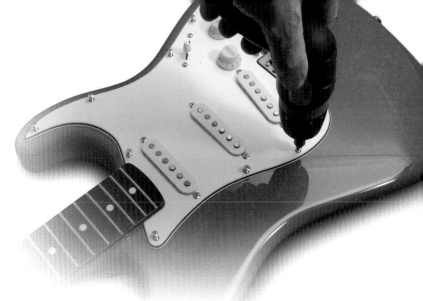

Proposed work

I thought I'd start by demonstrating a few distressing techniques, and leave it for you to decide the extent of distress you prefer. The relic/antiquing process is necessarily different for contrasting components:

- Wood requires abrasion and physical distress.
- Metal requires accelerated corrosion.
- Fingerboards require very specific localised abrasion to simulate a 'played in' feel.

Plastic discolouration is an art in itself, so I'm going to cheat and use the 'aged' plastics readily available on this budget guitar and from many parts suppliers, adding an additional bit of graphite 'dirt' for the sake of authenticity. However, if you feel you want to work on your existing parts these are some of the substances known to be used for plastic discolouration:

- A Scotch-Brite pad or nail buffer
- Kiwi brown shoe polish
- Leather dye
- Ritz clothing dye (yellow and sunset orange)
- A dirty hard rug
- Incense
- Cigarette smoke
- Beer
- Tabasco sauce
- Coffee grounds (wet)
- Tea
- Evergreen stamping ink
- Amber lacquer
- Touch-Up cabinet sticks

These all have varied effects and degrees of permanence – it's amusing sometimes when the ageing 'wears off' on some relics and reveals pristine white plastic!

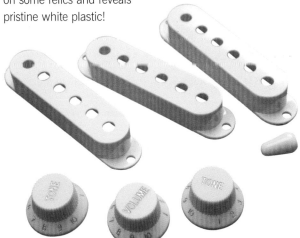

1 First disassemble the guitar – an electric screwdriver saves a lot of time.

2 A gentle waggle helps to remove tuner bushings.

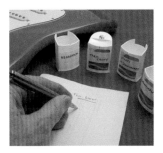

3 Keep a note of what goes where – a series of small resealable containers can be useful.

4 Keep a careful note of any neck pocket shims.

5 Carefully unsolder the jack socket and trem claw connections.

Bodywork

The body on this guitar is heavily coated with polyester, which by design is very resistant to extremes of temperature and will also take a lot of knocks and bangs. A real '62-era 'S' type would be finished in a far less durable nitrocellulose; the ageing effects here might include shrinkage and cracking, which is hard to simulate. I left this body out in the snow at –8° overnight and returned it to the drying cupboard three times, with absolutely zero effect!

1 However, losing the 'factory new' shine was easily achieved by a little light abrasion – I dipped a 1200-grit 'wet and dry' in a little white spirit to avoid clogging the paper and used a circular motion to lightly matt the surface. Screwing an old trem cavity cover and scratchplate in place means the 'ageing' effects will authentically only take place on the exposed parts of the body.

2 A little 0000 grade wire wool helps when addressing the more awkward corners and curves.

3 The removed trem cover shows the apparently 'oxidised' pattern.

4 The severe 'wear' pattern at the top bout was achieved with 320 grit freecut paper and a little more elbow grease.

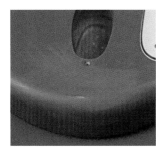

5 A similar wear mark near the jack plate could be elaborated with a few stage scars and dings.

A little 'dirt' simulation, achieved by rubbing in some graphite dust, will give a more believably aged appearance. The dings will be applied naturally and slowly by some regular gigging. This should put the dings in the correct places (guitar stand abrasion, etc).

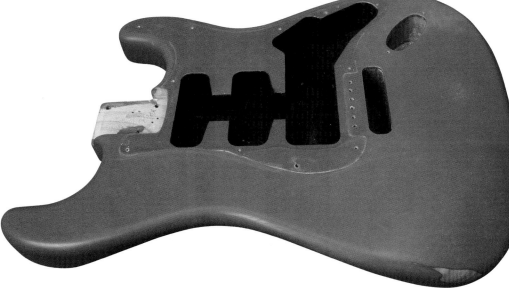

Oxidising the metal parts

On luthier John Diggins' recommendation I decided the safest approach to achieving a metal oxidisation effect was to use ferric chloride solution. This is readily available over the counter from 'Radio Shack'-type retail electronics outlets, and is sold as universal PCB developer. This liquid is corrosive, but controllable and safe if you take a few simple precautions:

- Keep out of reach of children and animals.
- Ensure adequate ventilation and avoid inhaling any fumes.
- In case of contact with the eyes, apply liberal amounts of water and seek immediate medical assistance.
- After skin contact wash immediately with plenty of water.
- Wear overalls, gloves and eye protection.

Separate out the parts for ageing. Generally, if the part has a direct mechanical function – such as a cog or bearing – leave it untreated, as you don't want any malfunctions, however authentic. Avoid threads and springs as much as possible.

1 I then lightly scratched the chosen metal parts by putting them all together in a Tupperware box and using the box for a little Samba percussion workshop (shake 'em up!).

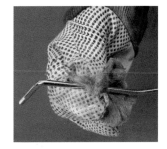

2 The brighter chrome parts needed a little direct wear from a paintwork abrasion pad and a little wire wool on the trem arm.

3 I then applied a little neat ferric chloride solution with a small brush and left the parts to 'corrode' for 20 minutes.

4 Pushing all the screw threads into a polystyrene block means only the heads get the ageing – authentic and desirable.

5 The tuners are only surface-aged and still work perfectly. The same applies to the other parts.

6 All the parts are then carefully rinsed in clean water to halt the corrosion process – take care not to immerse the tuners!

The neck

Even more so than the body, this is very glossy and looks a little unreal.

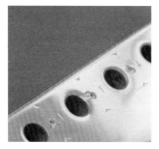

1 I first abraded the neck and headstock with 1200grit wet and dry, resulting in a nice 'feel'.

2 Again it's important to mask areas that wouldn't experience wear and tear.

3 I was also careful not to remove the transfers, as I'm not pretending this is an American guitar – it's clearly an 'import' and has a useful headstock truss rod access.

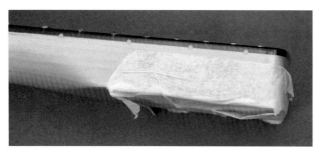

4 Sometime in a mythical '70s I let Eric Clapton play this guitar and he left his ciggy in the strings! Or was it a soldering iron?

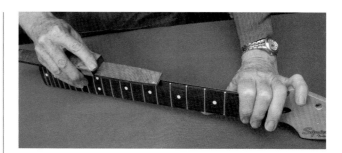

5 I rolled the edges of the fingerboard with a medium-grit file to get the 'played in' feel of Eric's 'Blackie'.

6 This needed a finish with a little 320- and 1200-grit paper.

The plastic parts

I chose this guitar because the plastic parts are already 'green mint' as supplied, but you can buy mint-coloured parts from any number of websites; or for a DIY approach you could try some of the solutions suggested above. However, plastics age in subtle ways and I doubt if you could better the proprietary custom-coloured parts available. What is needed is some abrasion – the new 'old parts' are very shiny and straight out of the mould.

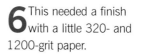

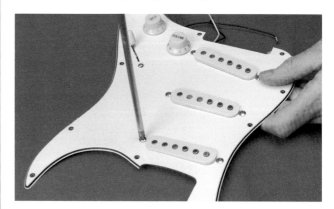

1 I disassembled the pickups with a No '1' Phillips.

2 I bagged up and sealed the pickups to avoid them getting covered in iron filings, and abraded the scratchplate with a players' plectrum pattern.

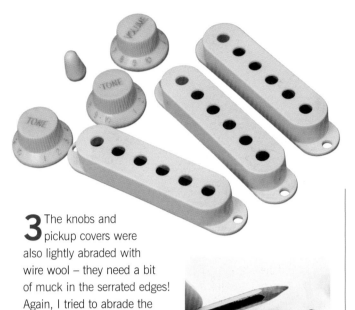

3 The knobs and pickup covers were also lightly abraded with wire wool – they need a bit of muck in the serrated edges! Again, I tried to abrade the pickup covers only where they surface. A little graphite from a pencil rubbed into the 'pick scratches' gives that ingrained dirt look.

If you really want to go to town you could replace the plastic wiring with some period correct cloth-covered push-back wire and the small pots with some CTS full-size types, etc – it's up to you!

The biggest giveaway in terms of period is the headstock truss rod access – I suppose you could go mad and buy a '62-style neck! I'll settle for changing the 'skinny' alloy trem block for a brass replacement from Guitar Fetish – this will improve the acoustic sound of the guitar, which always improves the amplified sound. The guitar also needed a new nut; the brittle plastic one supplied was unusually set too low. I'm building a bone nut from an oversize blank. See page 93 for more on nut work.

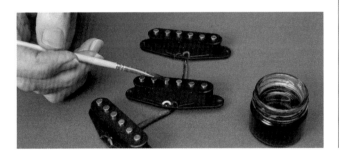

4 The pickup pole piece tops were given a light rust treatment with a dab of ferric chloride and rinsed fairly quickly.

■ The finished 'light relic' looks pretty cool and perhaps more appealing than an over-shiny import – the usual set-up procedures ensure it plays damn good too!

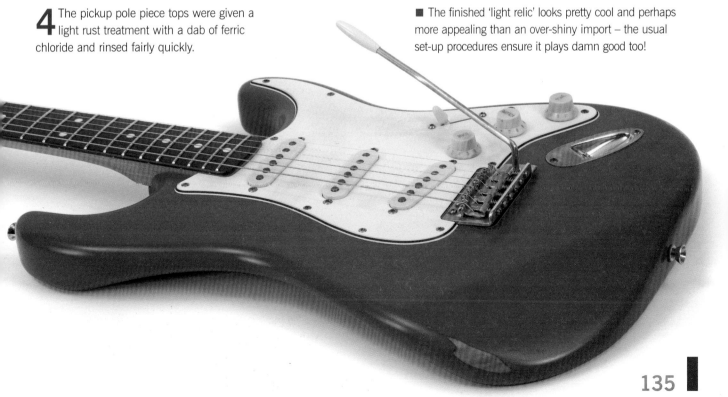

BUILD YOUR OWN ELECTRIC GUITAR

Our four project guitars

In the course of this book I've actually assembled and fitted three complete guitars and heavily modified an existing guitar in order to demonstrate the range of possibilities within the 'S' type formula. The '50s guitar is a classic of its time but is still a perfect pop guitar. The '60s guitar represents a 'modernisation', with a compound radius rosewood fingerboard and stacked humbuckers, making for a very practical stage instrument. The 'Maple' flame top is a very modern-looking and distinctive-sounding instrument. The heavily modified 'Dark Side' offers the potential of humbuckers and also an 'acoustic' bridge. You can mix and match all these possibilities to create your perfect guitar.

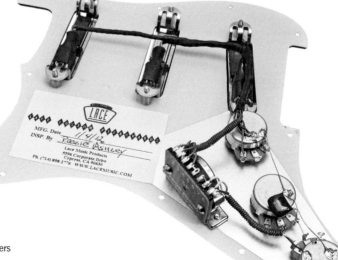

LEFT The push-pull tone pot offers a variety of pickup configurations.

RIGHT The pre-wired 'lace' pickguard.

'Buddy' – a '50s-style 'S' type

I'm sure many of us wish we'd been there when rock'n'roll was being invented and the classic tools of the trade were first played. If we were millionaires we might seek out the real thing, and if we won the lottery visit a custom shop; but as consolation we could make one of these. This gets us 'in the area'.

General description

With a two-colour sunburst swamp ash body and huge maple neck this is the guitar that propelled '50s pop, as well as some early Chicago blues. The guitar is a practical combination of near authentic ingredients with some 'ageing' patina.

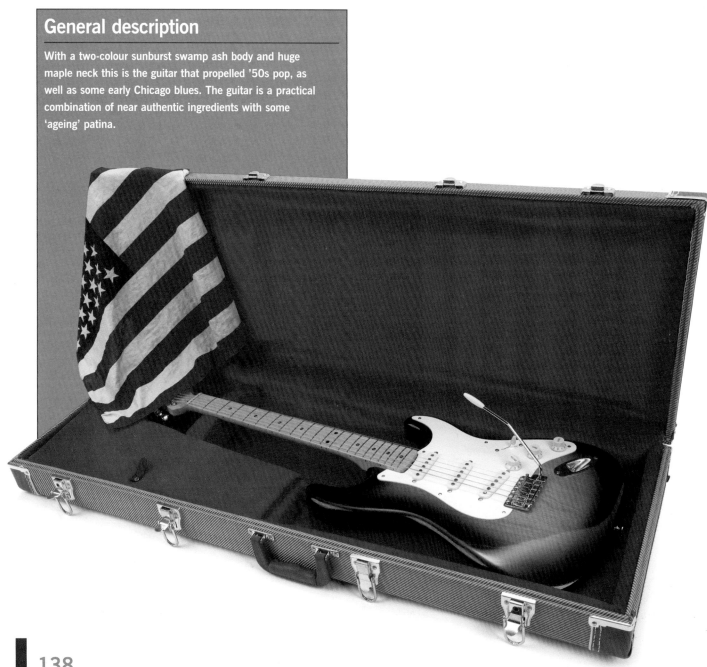

Making

As we've seen on page 78, this started out from a piece of ready-machined Stewmac ash which I supervised and finished in two-colour sunburst nitrocellulose in a pro spray shop. The very substantial licensed 'raw wood' Warmoth neck nitrocellulose was slightly tinted by John Diggins to give it an antiqued 'nicotine' finish.

■ The pots are '50s brass ferruled CTS types from Stewmac.

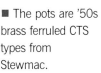

■ The electrics are wired '50s style except for the practical modernisation of a five-way switch. The generous body cut-out could accommodate any combination of pickups but I've gone for three 'vintage' single coils.

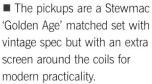

■ The pickups are a Stewmac 'Golden Age' matched set with vintage spec but with an extra screen around the coils for modern practicality.

■ The internal wiring is period cloth push back wire.

■ The pickup covers are JHS aged 'mint', and the Allparts pickguard remains white, as was the pattern with early plastics. The control knobs are sort of aged cream! These are all readily available, though early '50s rounded covers and low-profile controls are almost impossible to find.

■ I've added a layer of screening paint to the pickup cavity as a precaution against RF interference in modern gigging.

■ The trem tip is also a sort of green/cream – the overall effect is idiosyncratic, just like pawn shop guitars used to look, with plastics aged to different shades of white as their different compositions responded differently to UV exposure.

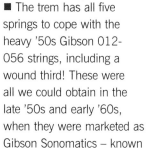

■ The straight-slot screws on the matching single-ply trem cover are unlikely to be seen on a '50s 'S' type, but they're a nice curio. With a little determination you might find straight-slot machine screws for the pickups and pickup selector.

■ The trem has all five springs to cope with the heavy '50s Gibson 012-056 strings, including a wound third! These were all we could obtain in the late '50s and early '60s, when they were marketed as Gibson Sonomatics – known colloquially as 'tow ropes'. They sound authentically wonderful for '50s pop and instrumentals; they don't 'bend', but that's what the trem was designed for! These new L5 strings are an improvement on the Sonomatics, which always had a very dull sixth string. The trem block is a heavy cast steel type – ideal.

■ The guitar has a vintage-style Stewmac trem and saddles. The bridge requires a No '1' Phillips for intonation and a traditional .50 Allen wrench for height and radius adjustments.

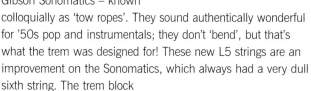

■ The guitar weighs a comfortable 7.5lb and the body thickness is a consistent 1.75in with heavy contouring.

BUILD YOUR OWN ELECTRIC GUITAR

■ The chunky 'boat' maple neck follows a typical 1950s profile with a substantial taper to the body. The scale length is 25.5in and the width at the nut 41.3mm. After my visit to John's spray shop I managed to scuff the neck during assembly, but a gentle abrade with some 3M paper and a little ToneTech clear gloss touch-up lacquer fixed that. Nitrocellulose can be a very forgiving finish – but take care not to inhale the vapour.

■ The string tree is a '50s-type ferrule with string grooves.

■ The integral fingerboard has 21 narrow gauge frets. The dot markers are black plastic.

■ The vintage-correct truss rod access is at the heel, requiring a 6mm straight-slot screwdriver and a temporary neck loosen.

■ The nut is a piece of antiqued bone. A little pencil graphite in the nut slots will help prevent tuning problems when using the trem.

■ The top strap button is in the eccentric early '50s location, which seems unusual to us now.

■ The machine heads are Stewmac vintage-style Kluson-alikes with a clever modern self-locking grip and a faux top slot.

■ The fingerboard radius is a vintage 7.25in, now matched at the saddles.

Signed off

I'm very pleased with this guitar – I could never afford a real '50s guitar, not even a reproduction, but I've managed to assemble and 'fit' a good working instrument which sounds and feels 'of the era'. It still wasn't cheap, as quality parts come at a price, but it's special to me and very individual. With its quirky screws and modern machine heads, no expert would be fooled regarding its authenticity for more than a few seconds, but that's as it should be – if you want the real thing that's also available, and I sincerely recommend what's on offer. However, if you have the time and patience give this DIY approach a go – I suspect you won't be disappointed. In June 2012 I used this guitar for its first gig (a '50s music celebration for the Queen's Diamond Jubilee). I did two sets in tricky stage situations – bright sunshine on an open platform, and a second set in a damp marquee. The guitar stayed in tune and sounded good. Result!

'Surf's Up' – a '60s-style 'S' type

In the '60s 'Chronic Blue' (as John Diggins humorously calls it!) became a classic colour, and though originally associated with surfing music this type of guitar came to be used for everything from instrumental pop to psychedelia, and is currently a fashionable 'retro' instrument.

General description

With an alder body, slim maple neck and rosewood board this is the guitar that suits every kind of popular music and a huge range of players. The guitar is made more practical with a combination of stacked humbuckers HX from Kinman, a modern Wilkinson trem and a modern compound fingerboard radius.

Making

This started out from a ready finished and licensed Warmoth alder body minimally machined for single coils.

■ The electrics are modern wired, with the practical installation of both a five-way switch and a 'hidden' push-pull switch for seven-way pickup selection (see page 64).

■ The nickel Phillips screws are period correct.

■ The guitar weighs a heavier than vintage 8.25lb, and the body thickness is a consistent 1.75in with heavy contouring.

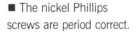

■ The pickups are Kinman 'Woodstock' stacked single-coil sized humbuckers in a matched set, with an extra screen around the twin coils for modern practicality.

■ The internal wiring is period cloth wire except for the pickup harness, which is PVC-coated and heavily screened.

■ The pots are still CTS vintage types – rugged and reliable. Except for the modern push-pull.

■ The pickup covers are Kinman white, and the '60s three-ply pickguard is softly aged. The controls are sort of 'aged' cream! These are all readily available.

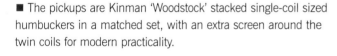

■ The guitar has a vintage-style but modern-performing Wilkinson trem and saddles with staggered string holes – simple but effective. The block is a heavy steel type – good for sustain.

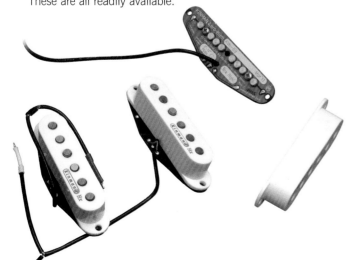

■ The trem arm is a modern push-fit and the intonation screws fit a No '1' Phillips or 3mm straight-slot (usefully versatile!). A larger than vintage and more robust 1.5mm Allen wrench is required for height and radius adjustments.

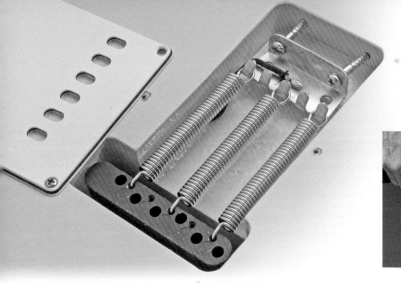

■ The trem has a three-spring arrangement commensurate with the light 'Nashville' plain third stringing, 009-042, as used by Hendrix and thousands of others since about 1966. They bend expressively and – if well set up – will stay in tune.

■ The slim 'C' maple neck has 21 frets and follows a typical 1960s profile with some taper to the body. The radius is a modern compound formula, 16in at the string-bending 21st fret and approximately 10in at the 5th position. The scale length is the normal 25.5in, and the wider than vintage width at the nut is 42.7mm. Usefully, this modern neck has a side access truss rod adjustment, but retains a vintage look at the nut. It requires a 3mm Allen wrench.

■ I masked the rosewood fingerboard at John Diggin's spray shop and he applied several coats of nitrocellulose on a turning spray jig. I had a go and feel I could do this now with some confidence. The important thing is to take your time, don't overspray, and do a light abrade between coats with some low-grit Free-Cut paper.

■ The rosewood fingerboard has 21 medium gauge frets. The simple dot markers are 'clay-alikes' in plastic.

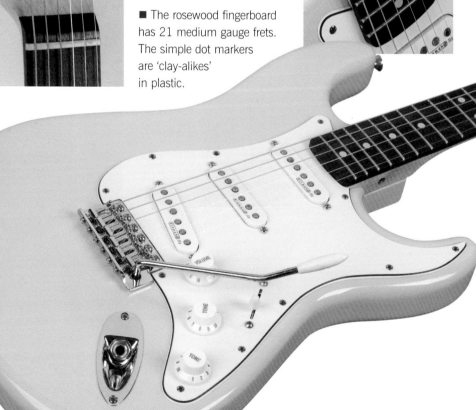

■ The string tree is a '60s-type seagull wing with a small 4mm spacer to raise it slightly – not putting too much pressure at the nut.

■ The machine heads are Wilkinson vintage-style Kluson-alikes, with options on the break angle offered by two different-height holes in the string barrel.

Signed off

This is turning into a very useful guitar. The Kinmans deliver a good, clear, bright single-coil sound, but with almost no electronic interference – brilliant.

The modern neck is of a type preferred by many players, and the easy truss rod access is a useful innovation. I like Trevor Wilkinson's ideas for improving the trem and tuners.

As with 'Buddy', no expert would be fooled regarding its authenticity for more than a few seconds, and once again the real thing is available if you want it and can afford it. But if you have the time and patience you should try this DIY approach. The results may surprise you!

■ The nut is a piece of antiqued bone. A little Lubri-Kit in the nut slots will help prevent tuning problems when using the trem.

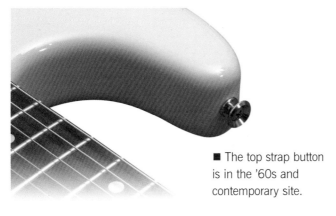

■ The top strap button is in the '60s and contemporary site.

'Tasty' quilt top – a modern 'S' type

The 'S' type has moved comfortably into the 21st century and continues to develop. It's hard to improve a classic without spoiling the essential character. However, I think this guitar managed to be different, but not 'OTT'.

General description

The idea for a tasty quilt top came from perusing a Stewart MacDonald catalogue: could I make a guitar that lived up to that sumptuous-looking body? In the end the combination of a maple neck and maple top with Don Lace Alumitone pickups makes for a very bright guitar – almost 'T' type bright – but excellent for cutting through horns and keyboards. This is a very modern-looking and sounding guitar.

Making

This is the easiest guitar of the lot to fit and assemble. It started out from a ready-finished Stewmac body machined for single coils or HSH.

■ The electrics are modern wired with the now standard practical modernisation of a five-way switch.

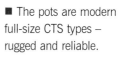

■ The pots are modern full-size CTS types – rugged and reliable.

■ The pickup covers are distinct and sort of 'Deco'.

■ The pickups are Don Lace Alumitones – his latest innovation pre-mounted on a pearlised fingerboard. This radical departure from pickup design is aluminium based, rather than copper, resulting in less resistance and higher output – a 'current-driven design' as opposed to the conventional voltage-based pickups.

■ The water-jet cut aluminium exoskeleton is mated to a micro winding using 90% less fine copper wire, creating a hybrid low-impedance/ high-impedance pickup.

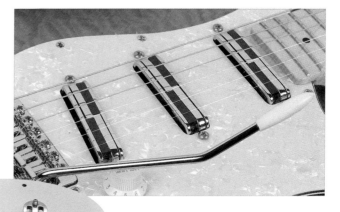

■ The guitar weighs a heavier than vintage 8.25lb, and the body thickness is a consistent 1.75in with moderate contouring.

■ The internal wiring is modern PVC-coated wire, including the pickup harness, which is heavily screened.

■ I did some work on the unshaped headstock at John's workshop. Using the Stauffer/Bigsby headstock shape is currently an infringement of a certain company's copyright, so I'm fashioning something else. As the guitar is so tasty I thought I'd take a bite out of the Stauffer shape.

■ The guitar has a vintage-style but modern-performing Wilkinson trem and saddles, with a GFS brass block – excellent, and good for sustain. The trem arm is a vintage thread and the intonation screws fit a No '1' Phillips or 3mm straight-slot (usefully versatile!). A larger than vintage and more robust 1.5mm Allen wrench is required for height and radius adjustments.

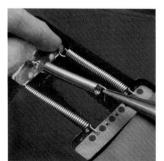

■ The trem has a modern three-spring arrangement commensurate with the light 'Nashville' plain third stringing, 009-042, as used by thousands of players since about 1966. They bend expressively and – if well set up – will stay in tune.

■ The slim 'C' maple Stewmac neck has 22 frets and follows a typical 1960s profile, with some taper to the body and a beautiful played-in feel to the rolled 'maple on maple' fingerboard edge. The radius is a modern and very flat 12in. The scale length is the normal 25.5in but with a wider than vintage width at the 42.6mm nut. There's a butt-end truss rod adjustment, therefore retaining a vintage look at the nut.

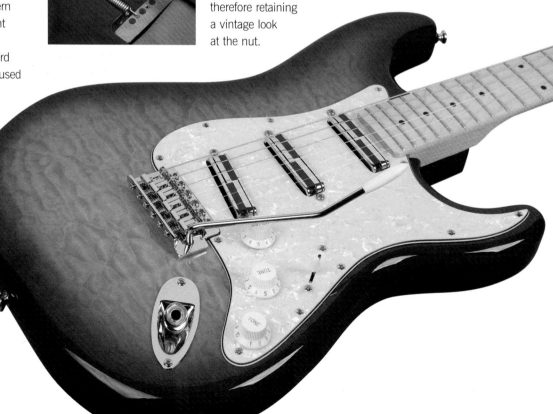

■ The maple fingerboard has 22 medium gauge frets. The simple dot markers are in plastic.

■ The string tree is a modern 'roller' type. Good for heavy trem use.

■ The nut is a piece of bone cut and shaped using the nut jig.

■ The machine heads are Wilkinson modern lightweight types with a locking bushing.

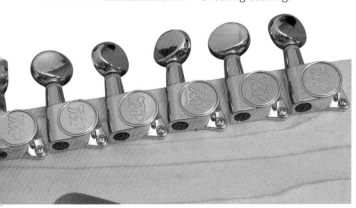

Signed off

The modern neck is of a comfortable 'rolled in' type, and the bright combination of maple and Alumitone pickups will appeal to many players.

This is a distinct 'S' type for the future. Why not dare to be different and give this DIY approach a go?

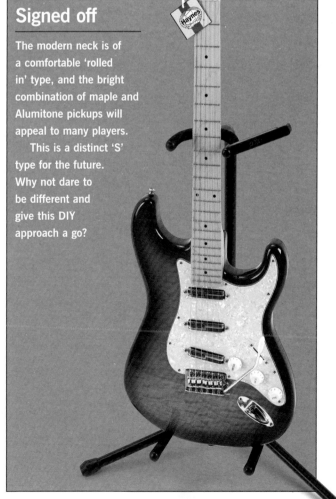

149

'Dark Side' modifications

One alternative approach to making your own guitar is to customise and improve an existing budget guitar. Every part you need is readily available, and it's very satisfying to create an instrument that reflects your character.

General description

This Chinese Squier featured in my very first guitar book in 2006 and plays really well. It's stable and plays in tune. I've taken the opportunity to try some radical changes in the pickup department, creating a very versatile guitar.

■ One popular modification I've tried is to add a humbucker to the single coils of the traditional 'S' type. See page 68. The thing to remember here is to balance your single coils to cope with the likely extra output of the humbucker. On this guitar I've added a couple of high-output Wilkinson single coils to match the Stewmac Golden Age PAF humbucker at the bridge.

■ I've also decided to try customising the guitar to a 'Dark Side' look with new accessories – a black pickguard, jack socket, tuners, etc – creating a very individual appearance.

■ I tend to feed the magnetic pickups to a conventional amp and the piezo bridge to an acoustic amp – which works really well. However, one important consideration with any two-amp set-up is avoiding 'earth' or 'ground' loops. You can either add 1:1 isolating transformers to your breakout box or buy in a really good splitter, such as this 'Dual' one from the German company Lehle, which has built-in transformers and earth-lift facilities as well as comprehensive stomp-box-like switching – enabling you to turn the two outputs on or off as required in your set, with a clear lighting indication of what's going where. Brilliant!

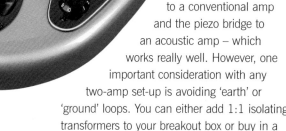

■ A separate volume control for the piezo is dual function, offering two EQ curves.

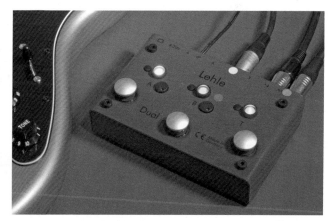

■ For performance the guitar also has a brass trem block – a big improvement on the old light alloy. The 'acoustic' piezo bridge is another popular modification.

Signed off

With very little machining the humble Squier has become a very versatile guitar. Note that the guitar now has two volume controls and one tone! The separate volume for the piezo is also a push-pull for optional EQ curves.

Appendices, glossary and contacts

What you will need most when building your own guitar, as I discovered, is patience. Nothing ever goes quite according to plan but, with time and determination, you can achieve a very personal guitar.

LEFT The heart of the Gretsch sound.

RIGHT Cigar box guitar by Tom Bingham of Corby, England.

These are all the essentials you'll need to order for an 'S' type build. Remember that second-hand and recycled parts can often look cooler than new!

- **Body** – Ash or alder with suitable cut-outs for your intended pickup arrangement. The body can be raw timber or pre-finished. Maple cap tops look cool.
- **Neck** – Usually maple with a choice of fingerboard radii from vintage to compound. Neck profiles also vary from boat vintage to super slim. Rosewood or ebony fingerboard.

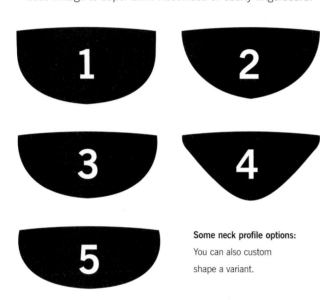

Some neck profile options:
You can also custom
shape a variant.

- **Pickups** – A myriad of options. Base your choice on the type of music you intend to make, from heavy metal humbuckers to single-coil sting.
- **Three pots** – Use the best you can afford and consider push-pull and taper options for versatility.
- **Capacitor(s)** – Consider the options – they can affect tone – and buy the best. Experiment with values.
- **Knobs, pickguard, trem tip** – White, black, cream, mint, gold or 'aged' relic?
- **Jack socket and retainer** – Go for quality.
- **Trem** – Vintage or modified? Usually best bought as a complete working package, as not all saddles fit all bridges. Springs should be included.
- **Trem cover** – Match to the pickguard.
- **String tree** – Vintage or modern?
- **Tuners** – Vintage or modern, but definitely lightweight for balance. Consider locking types.

- **Strap buttons** – Locking or standard?
- **Wire** – Push-back vintage is best and easiest to use. You need a metre of each of two colours.
- **Solder and tinner**
- **Nut** – Bone or graphite? Pre-shaped or a raw blank?
- **Screws** – Many components are supplied *with* screws.
- **Machine head:** wood screw – No '3' ⅜in round-head Phillips – steel nickel-plated.
- **Scratchplate:** wood screw – No '4' ½in raised countersunk Phillips – steel nickel-plated.
- **Neck plate:** No '8' 1¾in raised countersunk Phillips – steel nickel-plated.
- **String guide:** wood screw – No '3' ⅜in Phillips round-head.
- **Trem cover plate:** No. '4' ½in raised countersunk Phillips – steel nickel-plated.
- **Trem spring anchor:** No '8' 1¾in raised countersunk Phillips – steel nickel-plated.
- **Jack plate:** No '4' ½in raised countersunk Phillips – steel nickel-plated.
- **Strap button:** wood screw – No '6' 1in raised countersunk Phillips – steel-nickel plated.
- **Trem pivot:** wood screw – No '6' 1¼in round-head Phillips – steel nickel-plated.
- **Octave:** 4-40 UNC ⅝in round-head Phillips – steel nickel-plated.
- **Height adjustment 1 and 6:** 4-40 UNC ⁵⁄₁₆in socket oval point – steel nickel-plated.
- **Height adjustment 2 to 4:** 4-40 UNC ⅜in socket oval point – steel nickel-plated.
- **Trem arm thread:** 10-32 UNF (there are variants however).
- **Truss rod:** 10-32 UNC (some old truss rods were 8-32 UNC).
- **Trem plate to block:** 8-32 ⅜in Phillips flat countersunk – steel nickel-plated.
- **Pickup:** 6-32 UNC ⅝in raised countersunk – steel nickel-plated.
- **Pickup selector:** 6-32 UNC ⅝in raised countersunk – steel nickel-plated.
- **Nitrocellulose lacquer or Polyurethane** – If finishing the guitar yourself.
- **Strings** – Of your chosen gauge.

Suppliers and useful contacts

- www.Stewmac.com – Many thanks to Stewart MacDonald and especially Jay Hostetler, Jayme Arnett and Erick Coleman for making this book possible.
- www.Warmoth.com – Some fabulous bodies and necks by Sean Hosfelt.
- www.tonetech.co.uk – Luthiers' suppliers and specifically good for touch-up nitrocellulose supplies.
- www.JHS.co.uk – Makers of so many small parts and essential accessories, guitar parts and guitar tech tools.
- www.Lacemusic.com – Great pickups and advice on wiring.
- www.allparts.uk.com – A great source for those difficult-to-find components.
- www.draper.co.uk – Draper tools, for all the essential DIY supplies and routing equipment.
- www.clarkeinternational.com – Bench grinders and sanders.
- www.microplane.com – Microplane Tools, for brilliant wood-shaping tools.

- www.wdmusic.co.uk.
- www.graphtech.com – For 'Ghost' piezo pickups.
- www.schattendesign.com – Useful tools and patented guitar gizmos.

Lemon oil
- D'Andrea, USA from www.musicexpert.com.
- Dunlop www.jimdunlop.com.

Strings
- www.djmusic.com.
- www.daddario.com.

Plectrums
- www.jimdunlop.com.

Adhesives
- www.titebond.com.

Bibliography

Bacon, Tony, and Moorhouse, Barry. Many excellent guitar books, published by IMP and Backbeat Books.

Brosnac, Donald. *Guitar Electronics for Musicians* (Omnibus Press, 1995).

Burrluck, Dave. *The Player's Guide to Guitar Maintenance* (Backbeat Books, 2002).

Denyer, Ralph. *The Guitar Handbook* (Alfred A. Knopf, 1994).

Duncan, Seymour. *Pickup Sourcebook* (Seymour Duncan, 2005).

Erlewine, Dan. *Guitar Player Repair Guide* (Backbeat Books, 2007).

Foster, Mo. *British Rock Guitar* (Northumbria Press, 2011). Also visit www.mofoster.com

Hunter, Dave. *The Electric Guitar Sourcebook* (Backbeat Books, 2006).

Hunter, Dave, & Bacon, Tony. *Totally Guitar: The Definitive Guide* (Backbeat Books, 2008).

Oakham, Martin. *Build Your Own Electric Guitar* (Omnibus Press, 2006).

Osbourne, Nigel. *Totally Interactive Guitar Bible* (DVD, CD and book, Jawbone Press.com, 2006).

Schatten, Les. *The New Book of Standard Wiring Diagrams* (Schatten, 2008).

Glossary

Action – Word used to describe the general state of adjustment of a guitar in terms of playability.

Ball-end – Conventional type of guitar string end.

Bending – Pushing a string across the guitar's neck, increasing its tension and thereby changing its pitch.

Bigsby – A patented vibrato device developed by the late Paul Bigsby.

'Blocked off' – Term used to describe a tremolo/vibrato with a substantial wooden wedge behind the tremolo block.

Bout – Curve in the side of a guitar's body – upper bout, lower bout etc.

Capo – Abbreviation of 'capodastro', originally a Spanish device. A clamp across the strings of a guitar, shortening the effective sounding length for musical transposition.

CBG – Cigar-box guitar.

Earth loop (or ground loop) – A situation that arises when two pieces of equipment with earthed mains plugs are also connected by audio cables, effectively creating two paths to earth.

Effects – See 'FX'.

EQ – Equaliser.

F hole – A functional aperture found either side of the bridge on many archtop guitars.

Feeler gauge – A gauge consisting of several thin blades, used to measure narrow spaces.

Flame – A type of maple grain used on some guitars.

Frets – The narrow steel bars that divide the entire length of a guitar's neck.

FX (or effects) – Devices that manipulate a guitar's sound.

Gotoh – Manufacturer of a bolt-on vintage-like machine head introduced in 1981.

Ground loop – See 'earth loop'.

Grovers – Manufacturer of quality machine heads.

'Hard tail' – Modification in which the bridge is screwed down hard to the body, or the tremolo/vibrato is 'blocked off' by means of a substantial wooden wedge behind the tremolo block.

Headstock angle – The angle between the neck and headstock.

Heat sink – A means of drawing heat away from areas adjacent to components that are being soldered, often achieved by the use of crocodile clips or similar.

HSS – Humbucker/single coil/single coil pickup arrangement.

Humbucker – Double-coil pickups wired in opposite phase and physically arranged in parallel or stacked, to cancel induced low frequency hum.

Kluson – Type of machine head commonly found on vintage guitars and now reintroduced.

MIDI – Musical instrument digital interface.

'Nashville stringing' – Modification in which a banjo G string is substituted for a guitar's E first string, the E string subsequently used as a second string, the B string as its first unwound 'plain' third, the normal wound third as its fourth string, and so on.

Open string – A string sounded along its entire length (ie not pressed down to the fretboard anywhere).

PCB – Printed circuit board.

Phase reversal – When the polarity of a DC circuit is reversed, often in the context of mixing polarities – eg one pickup 'in phase' the other 'reverse phase'. The ensuing phase cancellation produces interesting and unpredictable perceived equalisation effects, infinitely adjustable by volume control adjustment on the individual pickups.

Pole piece – Metal pickup element that sits underneath the strings.

Pots – Potentiometers.

PU – Pickup.

Quilt top – A type of maple grain patterning.

Relic – New but convincingly 'worn-in' replica of a '50s or '60s classic guitar, with distressed body, rusty screws and faded pickups.

RF – Radio frequency.

'S' type – A classic American guitar design of the 1950s.

Schaller – A type of machine head.

Screen(ing) – Metallic shield around sensitive 'unbalanced' guitar circuits, connected to an earth potential to intercept and drain away interference.

Shimming – Adjusting the pitch of a guitar neck by inserting thin wooden shims or wedges in the neck cavity.

SLO – An 'S type-like object'. Every guitar manufacturer in the world seems to make one.

Solid-body guitar – A guitar without resonant cavities.

'T' type – Another early '50s American guitar design.

Tinning – Applying a little melted solder to an item and allowing it to cool. This minimises the amount of time that heat has to be applied when soldering items together.

Tone woods – Woods prized for their acoustic resonance.

Tremolo (or trem) – Misnomer for the vibrato, a lever attached to the bridge that's used to alter the tension and hence the musical pitch of the strings. Popularly known as a 'whammy bar'.

Tusq – Patented artificial ivory made by the Canadian company Graph Tech.

Vibrato – See 'tremolo'.

Acknowledgements

Many thanks to:

■ John, Andy and Mike Diggins, at
www.jaydeecustomguitars.co.uk, keep me on track
and put up with my 101 questions. I'm their sorcerer's
apprentice.

■ Clare Bartlett, PA to Brian May. Brian and Clare gave their
time willingly to this project. Brian is a gentleman and
scientist.

■ Peter Malandrone, guitar tech to Brian May, who gave
me much advice and guidance as well as contributing
equipment to my music charity. Many thanks.

■ Andrew Guyton (www.guytonguitars.com), for access
to his workshop, an interview and some fantastic 'Red
Specials'.

■ Shawn Leaver for giving me generous access to his 'Red
Special' and also a short interview.

■ Michele at Cgars (www.cgars.com), for supplying the
cigar box.

■ Judy Caine for Music On Earth management and photo
research.

■ Karl David Balmer for putting up with Daddy making a
noise and learning Rockschool 'Initial' – 'Five minutes a
day and you will learn to play!'

■ My mentor Brendan McCormack, for 43 years of
inspiration and endless patience. Special thanks to
his daughters Frith and Ana for Petersen's, lutes and
continuing mindscaffolding. The beat goes on!

Credits

Author – Paul Balmer

Editor – Steve Rendle

Design – Richard Parsons

Copy editor – Ian Heath

Studio photography – John Colley

Technical photography – Paul Balmer

Photo research – Judy Caine

Library photos – Getty Images (P6, P19, P118)

Index

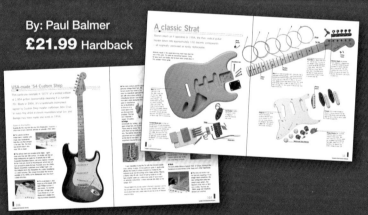
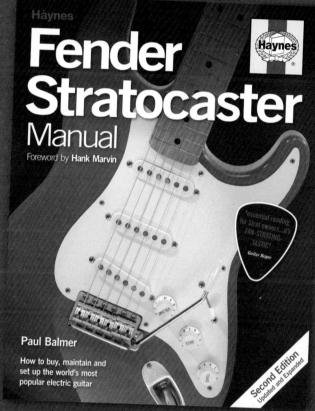